THE BOOK OF S

C000093691

SCARVES, SHAWLS AND TIES
DRESSED WITH IMAGINATION

Translated by Gabi Keller-O'Donovan

ON STREAM

Christiane Keller-Krische

HOBBY- UND FREIZEITLITERATUR

A book for all those who like creativity.

Editing, copy and text:
Christiane Keller-Krische, Gau Algesheim

Illustrations:
Ingrid Wanner, Mainz

Photographs:
Horst Bless, Worms
Anne Marie Pink, Ingelheim (p.165)

Black and White Pictures were provided by:
Co. Christian Fischbacher, Langenau

Design and Layout:
Werbeatelier Creative Media Design, Bingen/Rh

Lithography:
detepe MedienCom GmbH, Emmelshausen

Printing:
Schleunungsdruck Gmbh, Marktheidenfeld, Germany

The models outfits (Gabi Lauton, Kathleen Madden, Otto Kern, Strenesse, Tonga and Windsor) have been supplied by the boutique **MODISSIMA**, prop. K. Langer, Ingelheim.

Scarves worn by the models were supplied by:
Christian Fischbacher, Langenau
Codello Gmbh, Seefeld
Giorgio Passigatti GmbH, Neu-Ulm
Jammers & Leufgen GmbH & Co., Willich

Published 2000 in Ireland by On Stream Puplications Ltd. Clohroe, Blarney, County Cork, Ireland.
Tel/fax 353 21 4385798
email: info@onstream.ie. Website: www.onstream.ie
First published in Germany by Christiane Keller-Krische
© Christiane Keller-Krische

A CIP record for this book is available from the British Library

ISBN: 1 897 685 77 7

THE BOOK OF SCARVES: 100 IDEAS

Improve your appearance using clever ideas with scarves. This book will give you more than 100 valuable hints and suggestions on how to tie your shawls and scarves with imagination.

Step-by-step each movement is explained and easily copied by the reader. One idea follows the other in a logical sequence. Just a little bit of practice, and you will soon knot and tie your own creations.

This book includes ideas on how to use scarves for many occasions. For example:

- Scarves to add colour for leisure activities
- Scarves for the attractive business lady
- Scarves with a city look for a day in town
- Scarves to catch the eye at a formal occasion
- Scarves, cleverly combined with pearls and jewellery
- Scarves to highlight your hair
- Scarves as unusual belts
- Scarves for cheerfully cheeky children
- Scarves and ties for the fashion conscious man
- Scarves as light shawls on the beach
- Scarves as clever sun-tops

A cleverly tied scarf will add the finishing touch to your outfit. You will be delighted with your new appearance!

ACKNOWLEDGEMENTS

My sincere thanks to all those who helped in the creation of this book.

In my search for clever scarf-tying ideas I was ably assisted by Anne-Marie Pink and Metka Zimmermann.

Having read the first version of this book Heide Adomeit, Gisela Friesenecker and Barbara Memmesheimer gave me many useful ideas and suggestions.

My meagre sketches and drawings were patiently and magically transformed into clear illustrations by Ingrid Wanner.

Mrs. Langer allowed me to benefit from her professional advice when it came to combining the clothes and scarves for the photographs.

The scarves shown were made available for the photographs by the companies Codello GmbH, Seefeld, Jammers & Leufgen GmbH & Co., Willich 2, Christian Fischbacher, Langenau/Württ. and Giorgio Passigatti GmbH, Neu-Ulm, who selected them with great care and in accordance with my wishes.

Horst Bless ensured that the colour photographs were of good quality.

My parents and my sister racked their brains for a suitable title.

A lucky co-incidence caused me to meet Achim Stillert (Grafik-Designer AGD). Creatively he arranged every page of this book, and he delighted me with many good suggestions and tips. In this he was ably assisted by his partner, Markus Dehlzeit (Grafik-Designer AGD), and his wife Annette Stillert.

My very special thanks go to my husband Harro, for his never tiring encouragement and support in this project. For innumerable weekends he put himself in charge of the cooking and the care of our three small children, so that I would have hands and head free to produce this book.

Christiane Keller-Krische

How This Book Came To Be

Have you ever admired women who wore her scarf in a casual, yet very sophisticated way, and secretly asked yourself how this or that knot might possibly be tied?

For a long time I looked for clues to these secrets. Secrets which really are no such thing at all if you can find somebody who will, with a few turns of the hand, show you how to tie the most relevant basic knots.

On my travels I often noted the clever, feminine and sophisticated way some airhostesses tie their obligatory neckerchief – and many of them were quite pleased to receive an enquiry, not for a drink or one of the usual services, but for the secret of how their scarf was tied. In this way I got many a valuable suggestion!

I was surprised how easy it was it to tie my scarves once I had practiced a little. Being left handed, I had found it problematic to manage even a symmetrically perfect decorative bow. That was until somebody showed me the secret, and now I can do it,

even with my left hand!

In this book I would like to share all these little hints, tips and secrets. With practical, easy to follow and unambiguous illustrations I hope to demonstrate the basics of scarf-tying. I will show you fascinating, decorative (and feminine) variations on many of the themes and hopefully these will inspire you to create your own.

And if you already use scarves and shawls as accessories, you will be delighted with the variety of new suggestions.

I hope you will get lots of pleasure and enjoyment while experimenting!

Scarves - A Purposeful Fashion

In winter we drape long colourful scarves around our necks to keep them warm, and a headscarf prevents the cold winds from nipping at our ears. But come summer we can turn our scarves into colourful tops, cool skirts or a pair of Turkish trousers.

Scarves are 'in' – they add colour to any wardrobe and provide the finishing touch to any outfit. Wearing a cleverly draped scarf you feel more confident; others will marvel at your improved looks, and no one will be able to pinpoint how you did it.

Previously worn clothes get a new lease of life. A plain white blouse suddenly gains a certain 'je ne sais quoi'.

Have you spent a long and busy day at the office and cannot find the time to change for this evening's invitation? Dressed up with a smart scarf your practical office outfit will turn into elegant evening wear!

In many wardrobes are sad items that never see the light of day. The colour just doesn't suit you, though you thought it quite lovely when you bought the outfit. Bring it back into circulation! Surprise it, and yourself, with an uplifting scarf-idea. Suddenly you have so much more to wear!

Shawls And Scarves - A Little Guide

Before delving into the practical chapters of this book, let us first study some of the basics regarding shawls and scarves.

Shawls, kerchiefs and scarves come in a variety of shapes, lengths and sizes, and they are made from a wide variety of fabrics.

The most versatile and useful ones measure about 90cm x 90cm, but 70cm x 70cm is also quite an effective size.

Scarves smaller than 70cm x 70cm are difficult to knot around your neck – they are just too short. But they can look very pretty when tied into your plaited hair, or securing your ponytail.

Kerchiefs of 30cm x 30cm add a nice touch of colour when folded into your top pocket or when pinned to your collar.

The best size for a neckerchief is 28cm x 135cm. Shorter ones look nice in your hair, longer ones make attractive belts. If they are too wide they tend to 'take over', or they appear floppy, for example, when tied to form a 'fan'.

Frequently used fabrics are: Silk, Silkchiffon, Crepe de Chine, Silk Jacquard, Cotton, Wool, Viscose, Viscosechiffon and Polyester.

It is a good idea to choose the fabric of your scarf to match your outfit's.

Unfortunately, good quality shawls and scarves do not come cheap! But if you do not wish to spend a lot of money on buying a selection of scarves that match your outfits, invest in one good silken one. This should contain some of the colours that enhance your complexion and which are also found in many other items of your wardrobe.

Silk is easy to tie. It enhances elegant outfits, brightens your everyday clothes and even adds to a casual tracksuit. Silk is extremely versatile!

The colour of any scarf or shawl is extremely important if it is to be worn around the neck or draped around the shoulders. Before buying it, lay the fabric across your shoulders and watch the effect it has on your face.

How does the skin react to, and reflect in, the colours of the scarf? What does it do to your complexion?

Do you look attractive, does your skin appear smooth, are any wrinkles or shadows around your eyes fading? Is your appearance pert and cheerful? Attention should be drawn, not to the scarf, but to your face!

Or do you find that any lines around your mouth, eyes and nose have become accentuated? Do you look pale and unwell? Do you appear older or insignificant?

The scarf has hugged the limelight and pushed your face into the background!

We often know subconsciously which colours suit us, and which ones don't. Do not let yourself be persuaded to buy something in what is, to you, a new colour, simply so that you won't appear to wear the same things all the time. Pick colours that suit you and stick with them. This has the added advantage of allowing you to mix and match your garments.

Scarves can be plain, striped, chequered, printed with flowery designs – they come in a sheer plethora of colours and designs!

But some scarves that, on their own, look very attractive are not suitable for tying or knotting. The pretty design in the centre disappears with the first folding, and the plain coloured border may not go well with your other garments.

An exciting design with lots of detail deserves to be worn unfolded so that the pattern can be seen and admired. More discreet and simple patterns can be easily tied without losing their effect.

Before buying any shawl or scarf, gently tie it in your favourite style. This will quickly show you whether this would be a good purchase or not.

Labels And Instructions

Labels exist to indicate the quality, the fabric and to give washing instructions. They should not be viewed as an integral part of the scarf but should be carefully removed soon after purchase.

There are few things less pretty and more annoying than a label sticking out at right angles. It draws attention to itself and your artistically draped scarf fades into the background!

Some labels are stitched into the seam. Cut these off very close to the seam, using a sharp, small pair of scissors. Gently pull the remaining threads out of the seam.

Glued labels are more difficult to remove. Depending on the fabric it may be possible to use some dry-cleaning fluid.

Well Maintained For Extra Pleasure

Awareness of the basic rules regarding the washing and ironing of silk will give you lasting enjoyment of your favourite silk scarves.

Silk scarves can be hand washed in luke-warm water, at temperatures of up to 40°C. Always use a detergent that is suitable for specials or for delicate washes.

Never use detergent containing bleach!

Add a teaspoon of salt to the water. This prevents the colours from bleeding or running.

Gently squeeze the water from the scarf – do not wring it out! Wet silk is inclined to break, leaving ugly creases.

Neither is it advisable to just leave silk in water. Continually move the scarf – this prevents the colours from running into each other.

Rinse the scarf well, and add a squirt of vinegar to the last rinse. This highlights the colours and softens the fabric. Gently squeeze out the water once more, and then roll it into an absorbent cotton towel.

Gently pat the rolled towel – do not squeeze or wring it out!

You can iron your scarf on the off-side while it is still wet, with iron at wool setting.

You can also, of course, bring your scarf to the dry-cleaners. But it would be a shame if any harsh cleaning agents used there were to destroy or damage the silk's natural oils.

However, any item which you consider risky should be dry-cleaned. This applies especially to dark colours, which might bleed in the wash. And any scarf made from Chiffon, Satin, Georgette, and all men's ties, should definitely be dry cleaned.

Neckerchiefs which are worn close to the skin deserve special care. Avoid covering them unnecessarily in hairspray, deodorants or perfume. It is best to put on your scarf last, when all these have been applied and have dried.

THE PRINCIPLES OF FOLDING SHAWLS AND SCARVES

A scarf's size, its design and colours will determine how it might best be folded. Once folded, some of the colour will remain visible, the remainder will be hidden in the creases.

You can decide which colours and what part of the design should show. The way you fold the scarf will determine these effects.

The following pages will give ideas of how the same scarf can be folded in a myriad of different ways.

THE SQUARE

FROM A SQUARE SCARF TO A TRIANGLE

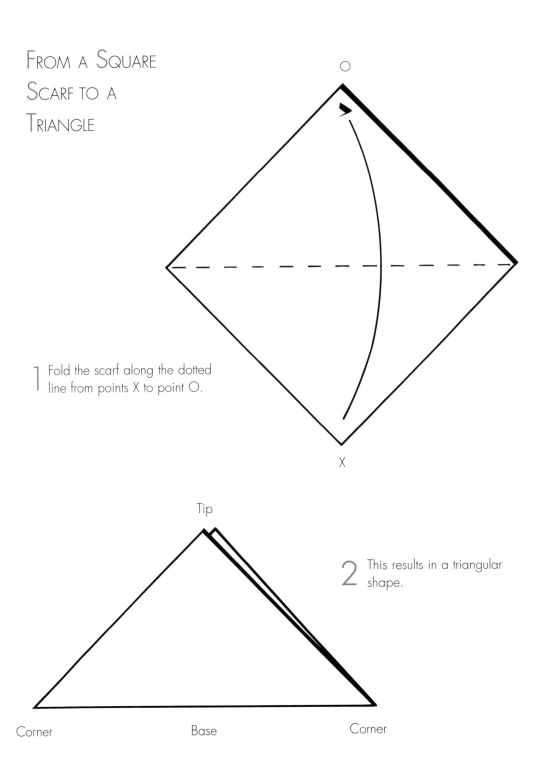

1 Fold the scarf along the dotted line from points X to point O.

2 This results in a triangular shape.

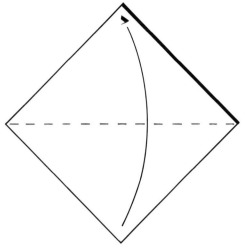

1 Fold the scarf along the dotted line.

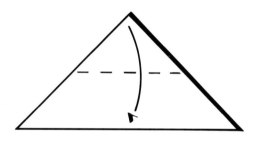

2 Bring the tip down to the base.

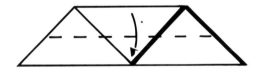

3 Fold the scarf along the dotted line once more.

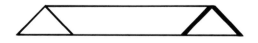

4 This results in a cravat.

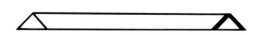

5 Repeat until the cravat has the desired width.

19

FROM A SQUARE SCARF TO A CRAVAT 2

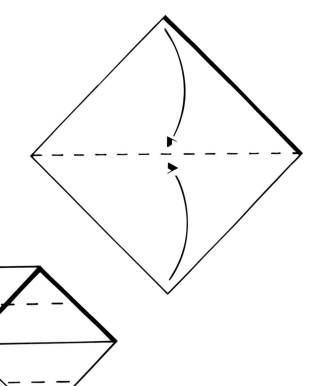

1 Turn the tips towards the dotted line at the centre of the scarf.

2 Fold the flat outer edges into the centre.

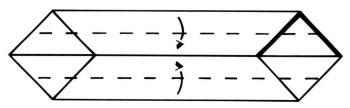

3 Keep folding the flat outer edges until...

4 ...the cravat has the desired width.

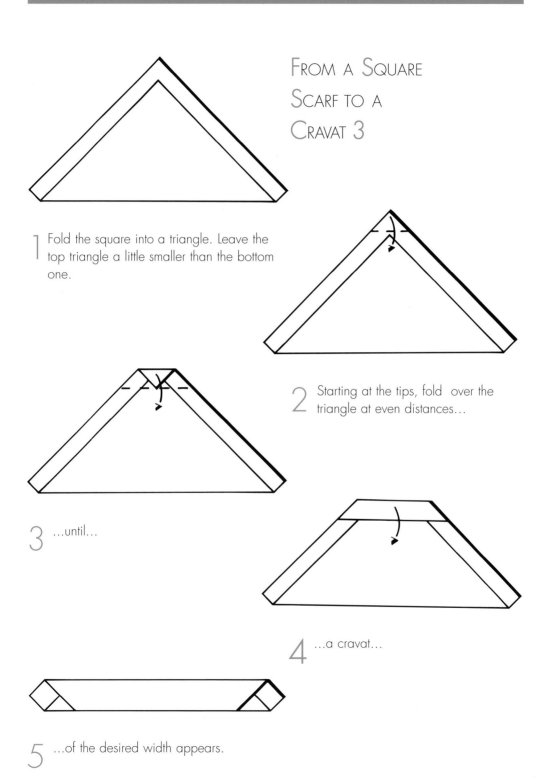

FROM A SQUARE SCARF TO A CRAVAT 3

1 Fold the square into a triangle. Leave the top triangle a little smaller than the bottom one.

2 Starting at the tips, fold over the triangle at even distances...

3 ...until...

4 ...a cravat...

5 ...of the desired width appears.

From a Square Scarf to a Ribbon 1

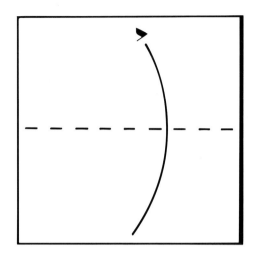

1 Halve the square along the dotted line.

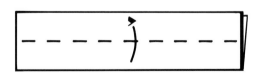

2 Continue folding the scarf in half until...

3 ...a ribbon...

4 ...of the desired width results.

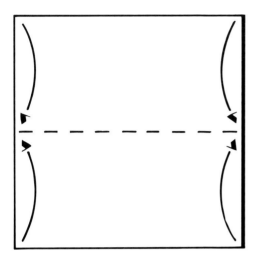

1 Bring the corners to the dotted line at the centre.

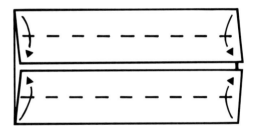

2 Continue to bring the outer edges into the centre until…

3 … a ribbon…

4 … of the desired width results.

Folding Rectangular Scarves

From a Rectangular Scarf to a Ribbon

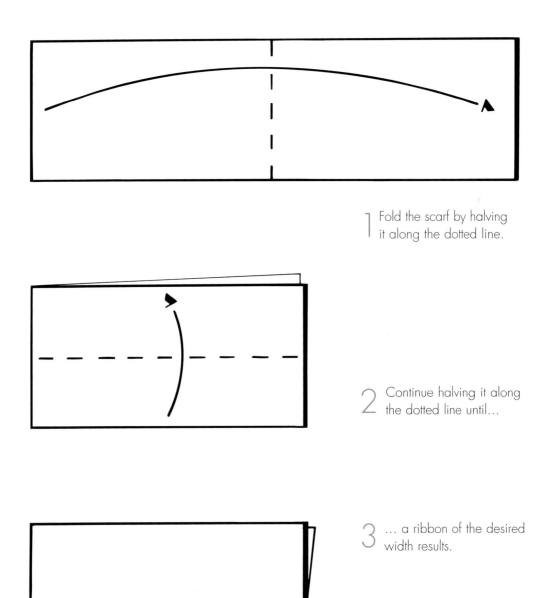

1 Fold the scarf by halving it along the dotted line.

2 Continue halving it along the dotted line until…

3 … a ribbon of the desired width results.

The Half Hitch

THE HALF HITCH

THE HALF HITCH FOR RIGHT - HANDED PEOPLE

This is the basis of many knots, and nearly everybody is familiar with it.

All drawings are inverted. Position the book in front of you against a mirror and tie exactly as depicted in the diagrams.

1 Position the scarf in a way that leaves two ends of unequal length. The longer end is for tying the knot.

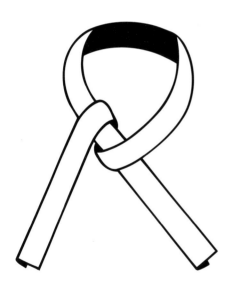

2 Hitch the longer end once over the shorter one.

3 Drape the longer end over the shorter one.

The Half Hitch is a decorative way of filling the open top of a blouse or a coat. It also looks quite pretty when worn on its own.

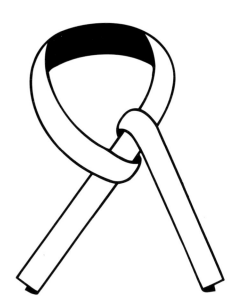

THE HALF HITCH FOR LEFT - HANDED PEOPLE

1 Position the scarf in a way that leaves two ends of unequal length. The longer end is for tying the knot.

2 Hitch the longer end once over the shorter one.

3 Drape the longer end over the shorter one.

This is the basis of many knots, and nearly everybody is familiar with it.

All drawings are inverted. Position the book in front of you against a mirror and tie exactly as depicted in the diagrams.

The Half Hitch is a decorative way of filling the open top of a blouse or a coat. It also looks quite pretty when worn on its own.

THE BASIC KNOT

THE BASIC KNOT FOR RIGHT - HANDED PEOPLE

The Basic Knot constitutes the basis for many other knots, and as such it is very important. It is formed by tying two Half Hitches, which results in a flat, straight, centrepiece.

All drawings are inverted. Position the book in front of you against a mirror and tie exactly as depicted in the diagrams

1 Hitch a slightly longer end over a slightly shorter one.

2 A Half Hitch.

3 Tie another Half Hitch over the lower, shorter end.

4 Tighten the knot by pulling both ends simultaneously in a horizontal direction.

The Basic Knot For Left - Handed People

The Basic Knot constitutes the basis for many other knots, and as such it is very important. It is formed by tying two Half Hitches, which results in a flat, straight, centrepiece.

All drawings are inverted. Position the book in front of you against a mirror and tie exactly as depicted in the diagrams

1 Hitch a slightly longer end over a slightly shorter one.

2 A Half Hitch.

3 Tie another Half Hitch over the lower, shorter end.

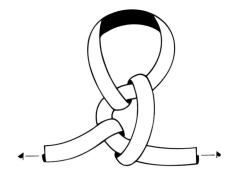

4 Tighten the knot by pulling both ends simultaneously in a horizontal direction.

THE BASIC KNOT

TWO LITTLE SECRETS FOR THE PERFECT BASIC KNOT

The most essential trick in tying scarves is knowing how to do the Basic Knot correctly. The end result should be flat and even. But it often behaves in an obstreperous manner, twisting and turning. These two little tricks will help:

BUT LIKE THIS !!

NOT LIKE THIS !!

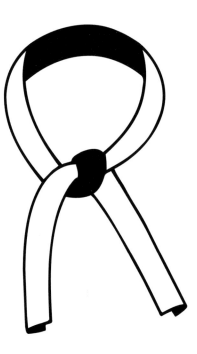

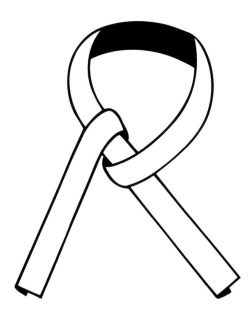

Hold this
end loosely

Keep this
end tight

1 Secret number one consists of not pulling on the upper, longer end, and of holding the shorter end quite tightly. If you pull on the upper end the knot will automatically twist and the shorter end will roll towards the front.

2 Secret number two is knowing that you must pull horizontally when tightening the knot, holding the left end in your left hand and the right end in your right hand. If you cross your hands while you pull, the knot will twist.

IDEAS FOR CLOSING

THE OPEN TOP

THE TORTOISE

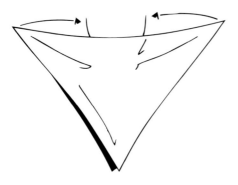

2 Bring the ends back to the front and use the Basic Knot to tie them under your chin.

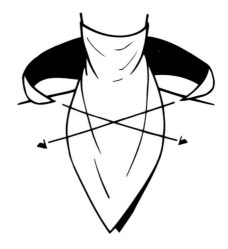

1 Fold a square scarf into a triangle and place it in front of your face under the eyes as if it were a veil. Cross the ends at the back of your neck.

3 Fold down the top of the scarf and use it to hide the Basic Knot.

4 Pull the Tortoise into a comfortable position and place the top of the triangle inside your collar.

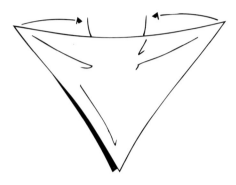

1 Fold a square scarf into a triangle and place it in front of your face under the eyes as if it were a veil. Cross the ends at the back of your neck.

2 Bring the ends back to the front and tie them with a Basic Knot.

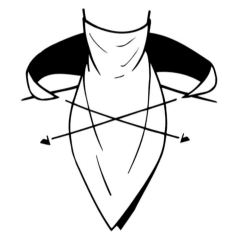

3 Fold down the top of the scarf, leaving the Basic Knot exposed.

4 Pull the Tortoise into a comfortable position and place the top of the triangle inside your collar.

COSSACK

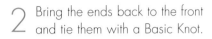

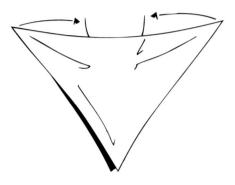

2 Bring the ends back to the front and tie them with a Basic Knot.

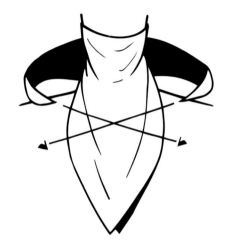

1 Fold a square scarf into a triangle and place it in front of your face under the eyes as if it were a veil. Cross the ends at the back of your neck.

3 Fold down the top of the scarf in a loose and generous fashion.

4 Pull the Cossack into a comfortable position and place the top of the triangle inside your collar.

ASCOT

Ascot

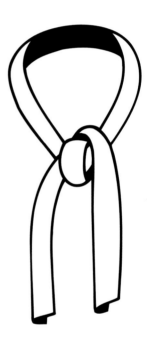

Who hasn't seen them – the displaced and dishevelled scarves which had earlier been so carefully arranged? Here is a way of putting an end to slipping scarves:

1 Lay the scarf around your neck and tie a Basic Knot. Leave one end longer than the other.

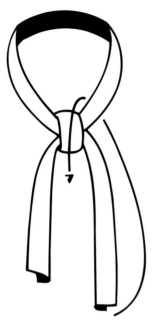

2 Use the longer end to make a Half Hitch over the Basic Knot.

3 Pull the top layer into a decorative shape and arrange it inside your collar.

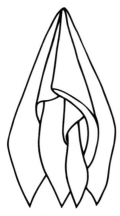

1 Hold the scarf by its centre and allow the ends to hang down loosely.

2 Push a small hair band, a shawl pin or a small curtain ring over the top of the centre.

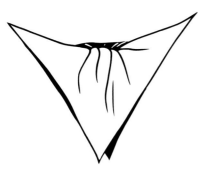

3 Fold the scarf over this knot, leaving the knot to point inwards. Catch the scarf at two opposite ends so that it forms a triangle.

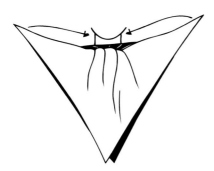

4 Loosely position the scarf at the front and tie it with a Basic Knot at the back of your neck.

5 Pull the scarf into a decorative shape and arrange it inside your collar, or allow it to hang loosely over the top.

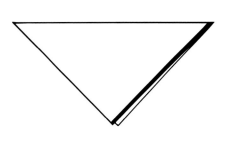

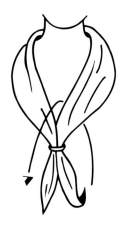

1 Fold a square scarf into a triangle.

2 Lay this across your shoulders and pull the two front ends through a ring.

3 Use the top end to make a Half Hitch.

4 Pull the scarf into a decorative shape and arrange it inside your collar.

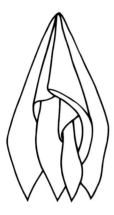

1 Hold the scarf by its centre and allow the ends to hang down loosely.

2 Tie a small knot at the top of the centre your are holding.

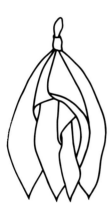

3 Catch the scarf at two opposite corners.

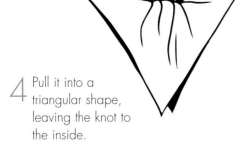

4 Pull it into a triangular shape, leaving the knot to the inside.

5 Loosely position the scarf at the front and tie it with a Basic Knot at the back of your neck.

Pull the scarf into a decorative shape and arrange it inside your collar, or allow it to hang loosely over the top.

LOOPS

LOOSE LOOP

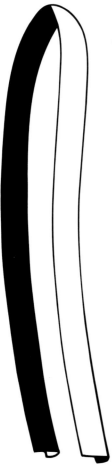

1 Halve a long scarf lengthways.

2 Lay it across your shoulders and make a Half Hitch, using the looped end at the outside.

3 Position the loop to hang loosely over the other two open ends.

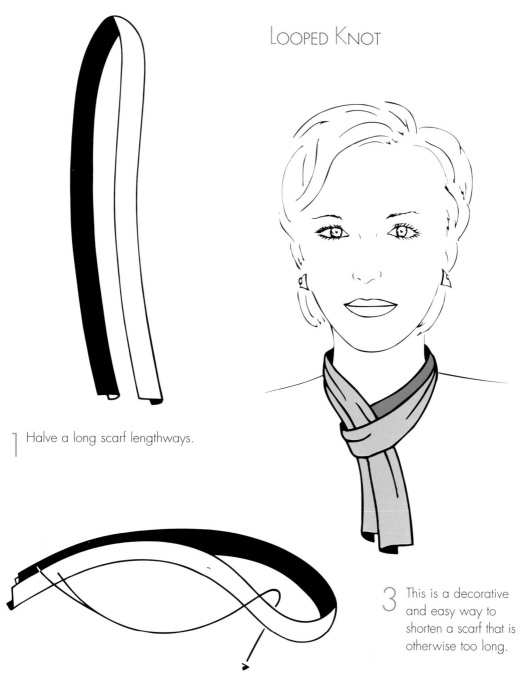

LOOPED KNOT

1 Halve a long scarf lengthways.

2 Lay it across your shoulders and pull both open ends through the loop.

3 This is a decorative and easy way to shorten a scarf that is otherwise too long.

CATERPILLAR LOOP

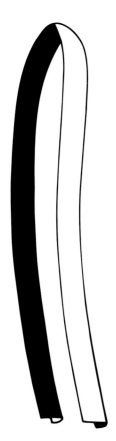

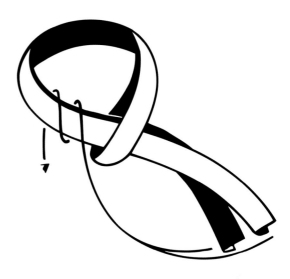

1 Halve a long scarf lengthways.

3 Wrap the two open ends a few times around the necklace.

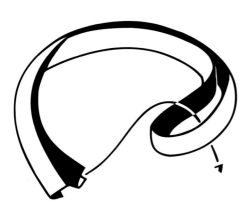

2 Pull the ends through the loop.

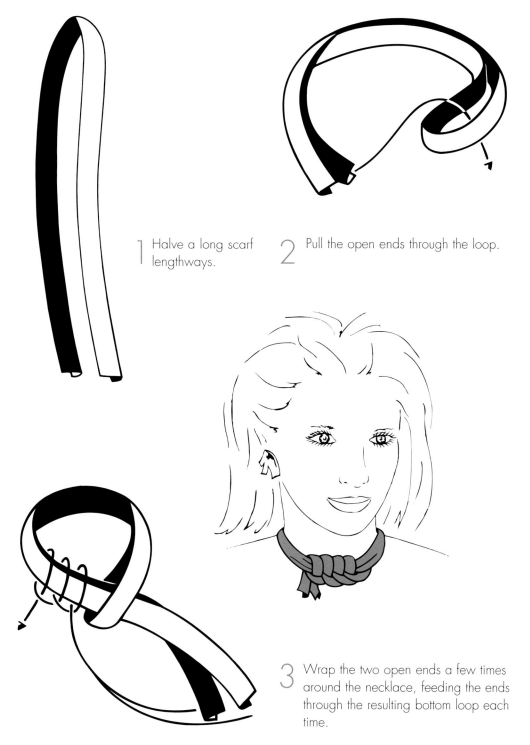

1 Halve a long scarf lengthways.

2 Pull the open ends through the loop.

3 Wrap the two open ends a few times around the necklace, feeding the ends through the resulting bottom loop each time.

Woven Loop

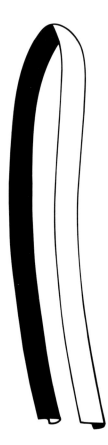

1 Halve a long scarf or light pashima lengthways.

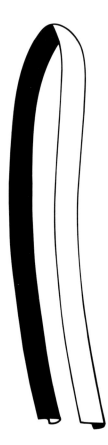

2 Lay the scarf across your shoulders and thread the open ends through the loop, one from the top and one from the bottom, just as if you were weaving.

3 Pull this creation into a loose and decorative shape.

This prevents your loops from slipping.

1 Form a looped knot.

2 Hitch the lower, longer one of the two open ends from underneath over the loop and…

3 …leave it to hang loosely over the top.

4 Next make a Half Hitch over what is now the lower end and tighten the knot by pulling horizontally.

NB:

The two tricks which apply to making a proper Basic Knot (p. 30) also come in handy here.

THE LONG SCARF

LONG BUT NOT LANKY

Lay a long scarf across your shoulders and tuck it under your belt at the front. For a pashmina, allow the width of the scarf to drape over the shoulders and stretch down into the belt.

Lay a long and soft scarf across your shoulders and simply tie a knot into each front end.

THE TRICK WITH THE BUCKLE

Lay a scarf across your shoulders and pull both ends through a pretty buckle.

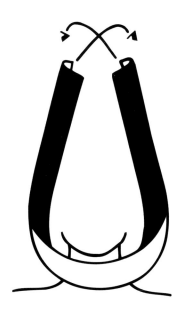

The ideal way to shorten a long scarf.

1 Place the scarf in front of your neck.

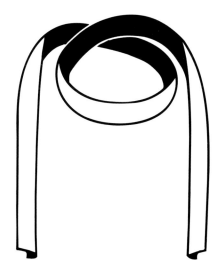

2 Criss-cross the ends at the back of your neck and bring them to the front again.

3 Tie the scarf, using a Basic Knot.

CAPRICE

1 Place the scarf in front of your neck.

 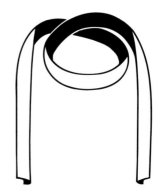

2 Criss-cross the ends at the back of your neck and bring them to the front again. Gently pull down the centre of the scarf in front until it forms a loop.

3 Cross the ends under the loop.

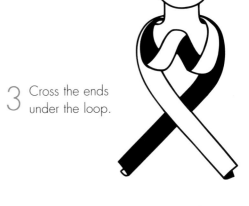

4 Drape the loop over the crossed ends.

5 Tie the ends above the loop, using a Basic Knot.

COME ON, LET'S TWIST!

SNAKE

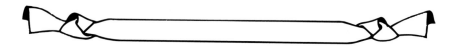

1 Tie a knot at both ends of the scarf.

2 Twist the scarf around itself and continue to do so until it looks like a twisted rope.

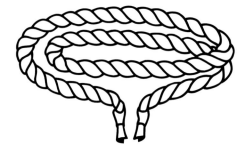

3 Wrap this rope around your neck once or twice, depending on how long it is. Leave the ends to point to the front.

4 Push the ends under the loop around your neck and leave one end to hang under the loop with the other hanging over it.

1 Twist the scarf around itself until it forms a tightly twisted rope.

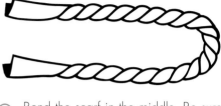

2 Bend the scarf in the middle. Be sure to hold both ends tightly at all times.

3 Hold both loose ends in the one hand and the rope will slowly unwind.

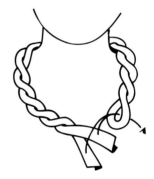

5 …and thread the two loose ends through the loop.

4 Place the rope across your shoulders …

6 Tie the ends using a Loopholder (p. 47), and if you have enough of the scarf left, tie them further, forming a Bowtie or a Rosette.

Twin Coloured Rope

1 Take two scarves of complimentary colours and tie them together.

2 Twist the scarves into a rope. Ideally you need a second person to hold on to the knotted end, but if no assistant is available just loop it over a door handle.

3 Place the rope across your shoulders and thread the two ends through the gap behind the knot.

4 Tie the ends with a Loopholder (p. 47), hiding the knot while doing so.

THE ROSE

This is where your scarf reaches elevated status. The Rose appears fascinatingly feminine and romantic. It looks so complicated, yet it is so simple!

Scarves of a dimension 40 x 120cm and soft shawls of 90 x 90cm are most suitable for the Rose.

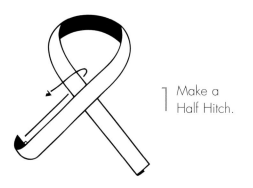

1 Make a Half Hitch.

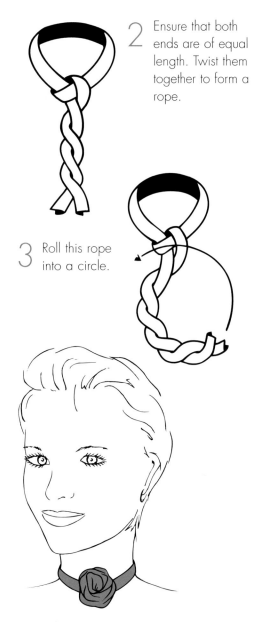

2 Ensure that both ends are of equal length. Twist them together to form a rope.

3 Roll this rope into a circle.

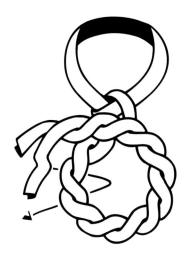

4 Gently pull a small pleat from near the ends and push this through the centre of the circle.

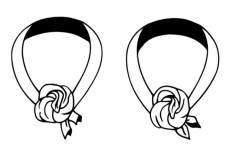

5 Hide the ends or leave the tips to protrude, like leaves.

CROCHET DOLL

For long scarves and largish shawls.

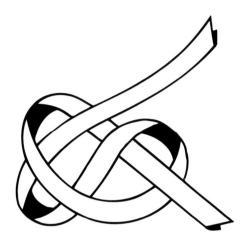

1 Form a small loop with the shorter end. Push two fingers underneath the loop and pull approx. 3cm of the longer end through the gap.

2 This results in a second loop – just as if you were crocheting.

3 Crochet on, and pull the end of the scarf through the last loop.

4 Tie this crochet-scarf around your neck, using the Basic Knot.

CROCHET SCARVES

TWIN COLOURED CROCHET SCARF

This is particularly effective where two plain coloured scarves of complimentary shades are used.

1 Knot the two scarves together.

2 Wrap them around each other once. This will form a loop. Pull the upper scarf through this loop, thus for-ming a second loop.

3 Form a third loop, using the second scarf.

4 Crochet on, and pull the remaining end completely through the last loop.

5 Tie the twin coloured crochet scarf around your neck, using the Basic Knot.

Bows

Half Bow

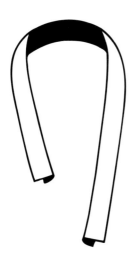

2 Form a loop out of the longer end and wrap the shorter end once around this loop

1 Lay a folded scarf across your shoulders. Leave one end slightly longer than the other.

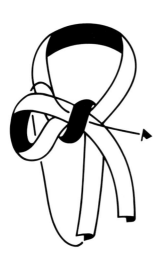

3 Tighten the bow by bringing the shorter end behind the loop and threading it through the flat knot at the centre.

4 Pull the Half Bow into a decorative shape.

1 Lay a folded scarf across your shoulders. Leave one end slightly longer than the other.

Bow I

Here are some hints for tying a pretty bow:
Always use the lower end to form the first loop.
Do not make too large a bow, and always tighten it by pulling horizontally.

2 Use this longer end to form a Half Hitch.

3 Form a loop out of the lower end.

4 Take a good hold of the lower loop.

5 Bring the upper end above the lower loop and form a second loop. Tighten the bow by pulling in a horizontal direction.

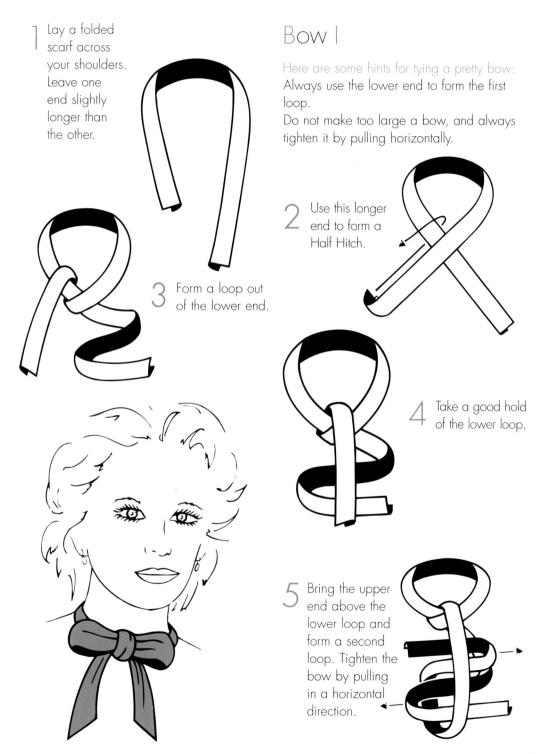

Bows

Bow II

Here is another way of tying an attractive bow:

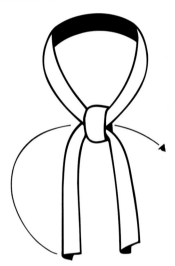

1 Tie a Basic Knot.

2 Pull the right end through the knot and leave a small loop.

3 Pull the left end through the knot in the same way. Then tighten the bow by pulling in a horizontal direction.

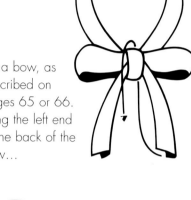

Bow Holder

The bow will keep its decorative shape if you secure it with a Half Hitch.

1 Tie a bow, as described on pages 65 or 66. Bring the left end to the back of the bow…

2 … and hitch it over the centre knot.

3 Then wrap it once around the right end and tighten by pulling both ends horizontally.

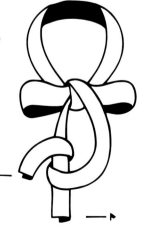

Bows

Rosette

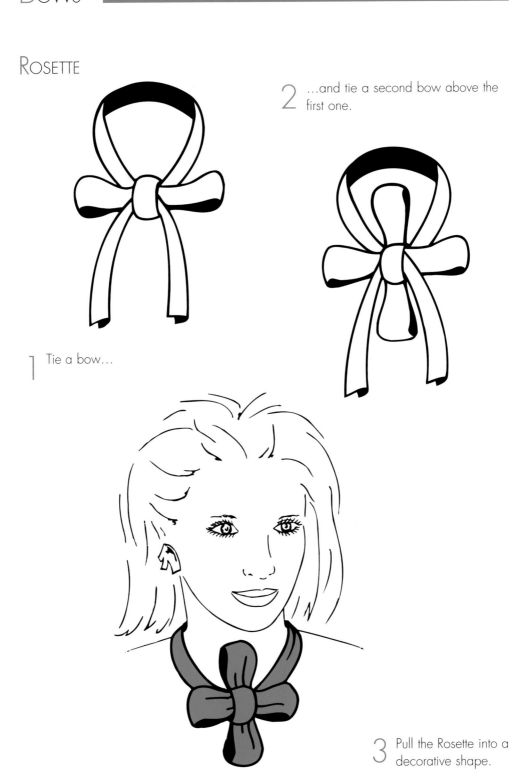

1 Tie a bow...

2 ...and tie a second bow above the first one.

3 Pull the Rosette into a decorative shape.

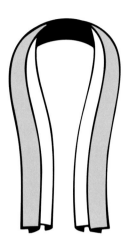

Twin Coloured Bow

To obtain a really cute looking Double Bow combine a plain coloured scarf with a patterned one of a complimentary colour.

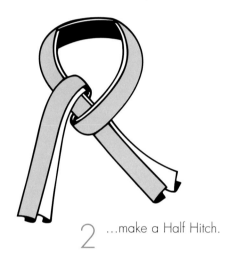

1 Lay both scarves across your shoulders and…

2 …make a Half Hitch.

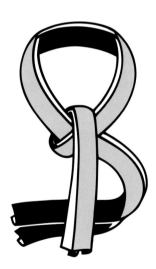

3 Use both lower ends to form a loop.

4 Use the other ends to form a second loop and tighten the Bow by pulling horizontally.

The Fan -
Stylish And Elegant

The Fan catches the eye. It makes you look special, giving you a decorative, individualistic and self-assured air. You will undoubtedly be asked how you managed to convert your scarf to such an interesting accessory. Even if the approach is not as direct you will quite likely notice the admiring glances in your direction.

On the following pages there are 9 different ways of tying a Fan. Select some that suit your scarf and have fun experimenting to find the way that looks best.

If you use your scarf folded into a Ribbon start directly at one of the ends and fold it into even creases. If you have formed a Cravat begin to fold the creases a small distance above the tip.

Very suitable for a Fan are scarves that have been folded into a Cravat of a width of 12 to 15 cm.

But a long scarf, 10 to 12 cm wide and 135 cm long, can give an even nicer result. Scarves that are wider than 20 cm tend to look sloppy.

A little spray-on starch (carefully) applied to the scarf may make it easier to handle.

And another hint: The best results are obtained with scarves of plain coloured sides, or with those that have a plain stripe along the edge.

The most difficult aspect of this creation is the neat and precise folding of the creases. But a small bit of practice will make perfect!

CARMEN

FOR RIGHT - HANDED PEOPLE

The Fan is festive and elegant and will draw all eyes towards you.

All drawings are inverted. Position the book in front of you against a mirror and tie exactly as depicted in the diagrams.

1 Lay a long scarf across your shoulders. Leave one end longer than the other. Make a Half Hitch.

2 Softly pleat the longer end into folds of about 2 cm each.

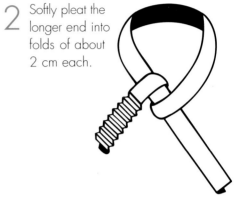

3 Depending on the length, wrap the shorter end one or more times around the pleats…

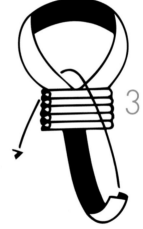

4 …and pull it through the front of the knot. Then pull the Fan into a decorative shape.

For Left - Handed People

The Fan is festive and elegant and will draw all eyes towards you.

All drawings are inverted. Position the book in front of you against a mirror and tie exactly as depicted in the diagrams.

1 Lay a long scarf across your shoulders. Leave one end longer than the other. Make a Half Hitch.

3 Depending on the length, wrap the shorter end one or more times around the pleats…

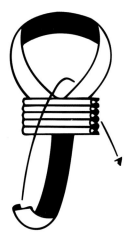

2 Pleat the longer end into folds of about 2 cm each.

4 …and pull it through the front of the knot. Then pull the Fan into a decorative shape.

FLAMENCO

FOR RIGHT - HANDED PEOPLE

All drawings are inverted. Position the book in front of you against a mirror and tie exactly as depicted in the diagrams.

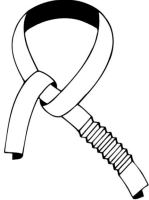

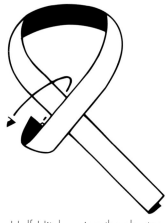

1 Make a Half Hitch, using the shorter end.

2 Pleat the longer end until you come to the Half Hitch.

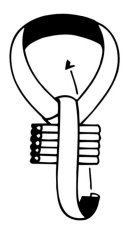

3 Pull the shorter end over the pleats and back through the loop around your neck.

4 Pull the lower end through the front of the knot and bring it back behind the loop. Then pull the Fan into a decorative shape.

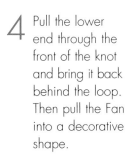

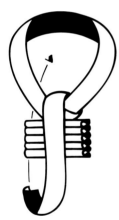

For Left - Handed People

All drawings are inverted. Position the book in front of you against a mirror and tie exactly as depicted in the diagrams

1 Make a Half Hitch, using the shorter end.

2 Pleat the longer end until you come to the Half Hitch.

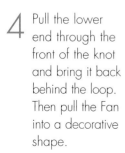

3 Pull the shorter end over the pleats and back through the loop around your neck.

4 Pull the lower end through the front of the knot and bring it back behind the loop. Then pull the Fan into a decorative shape.

CABARET

WHEN TIME IS OF THE ESSENCE

1   Pleat one end of your scarf, but leave approx. 45 cms unpleated.

2   Knot the loose end around the pleats.

3   This results in a ready-made fan.

4   Put the scarf around your neck and pull the loose end through the knot. Make a Half Hitch and tighten it, using the Basic Knot.

5   Turn the fan so that the end is hidden and pull it into a decorative shape.

1 Use the large scarf…

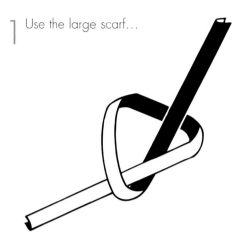

WHEN TIME IS OF THE ESSENCE

You will need a large and a small scarf of complimentary colours

2 … and tie a simple knot.

3 Pleat the small scarf into a fan.

4 Push the fan through the knot.

5 Tie the Fan around your neck with a Basic Knot.

This is easily prepared in advance. Just put it on when the time is right.

Accordion

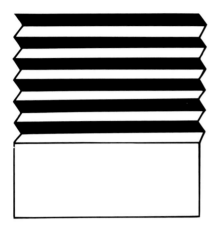

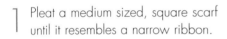

1 Pleat a medium sized, square scarf until it resembles a narrow ribbon.

2 Lay this pleated ribbon across your shoulders. Take care to keep the folds tightly closed.

3 Tie the pleated ribbon at the front, using a Basic Knot.

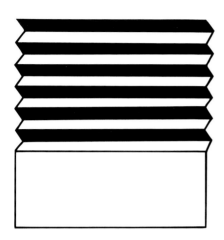

1 Pleat a medium sized, square scarf until it resembles a narrow ribbon.

2 Lay this ribbon across your neck and tie a Half Hitch.

3 Use a decorative pin or a nice brooch to hold the scarf at the front.

DRAGONFLY

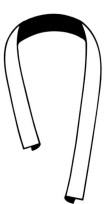

1 Lay the scarf across your neck, leaving one end longer than the other.

2 Tie a loose, slip knot into the shorter end.

3 Pleat the longer end.

4 Make sure to hold the pleats tightly closed at one side while pushing them halfway through the knot.

5 Tighten the knot and pull the Fan into a decorative shape.

Depending on the length of your scarf you can position the Dragonfly at the front of your neck or, for a more casual effect, further down your chest.

IMAGINATIVE USE OF

You'll look the height of fashion when wearing a combination of pearls and scarves, cleverly intertwined. Pearls are in - and imitation ones will do just fine.

PEARLS AND JEWELLERY

CORDOBA

1 Tie a slip knot into a long scarf or into a square one which you have folded into a ribbon.

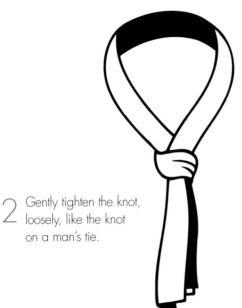

2 Gently tighten the knot, loosely, like the knot on a man's tie.

3 Thread a long pearl necklace through the loop.

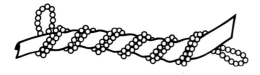

1 Twist a long scarf and a pearl necklace together to form a rope.

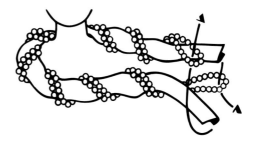

2 Lay this around your neck and pull the ends of the scarf through the opposite loops of the pear necklace.

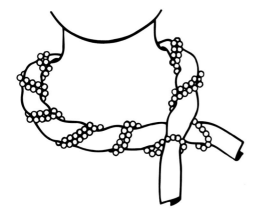

3 Use the upper end to make a Half Hitch and tie both ends, using the Basic Knot.

4 Leave the ends to fall down decoratively, or, if the scarf is long enough, tie them into a Bow, a Rosette or a Rose.

85

PEARLY FAN

This is a guaranteed eye-catcher! A scarf and a short pearl necklace are creatively intertwined, and the ends of the scarf are then tied to form a handsome Fan.

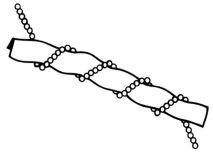

1 Take a long scarf or use a square one which you have folded into a ribbon. Twist this and a short pearl necklace together to form a rope.

2 Lay this rope around your neck and close the catch on the pearl necklace. Tie a Half Hitch, using the longer end of the scarf.

3 Pleat the longer end …

4 … and pull the shorter end over the pleats, forming a Half Hitch.

5 Bring the shorter end once more through the front of the knot. Pull the Fan into a decorative shape.

ONE, TWO, THREE, FOUR, FIVE

MAKE ALL OF YOUR
SCARVES COME ALIVE!

DUET

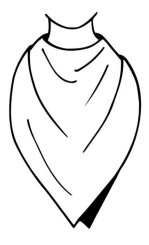

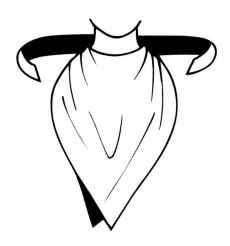

3 ... using the Basic Knot.

1 Drape a triangular scarf around your front and tie it at the back of the neck.

2 Take a second scarf of a complimentary colour. Fold it into a Cravat and bring it from the back, tying it at the front.

90

1 Use the Basic Knot to tie both ends of two scarves together.

2 Wear one knot on each shoulder, or bring one to the front and the other to the back.

RAPUNZEL

Take three matching scarves and knot them together. Then braid them into a loose plait, tying a knot at the second end.

SOME MORE

SASSY SCARF IDEAS

SAILOR'S COLLAR

1 Fold a square scarf in half.

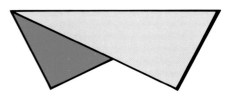

2 Lift the scarf at two opposite ends. This will form two triangles, one on top of the other.

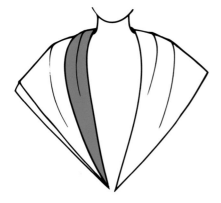

3 Lay these across your shoulders, the two triangles to the front, making sure they both remain of an even size.

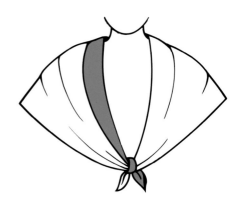

4 Tie a Basic Knot.

5 You can wear this knot to the front, at the back, or to one side, as you fancy.

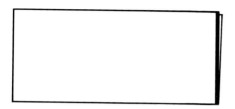

1 Fold a square in half.

2 Lay it around your shoulders, bringing the open end to the front. Tie the upper two corners together, using the Basic Knot.

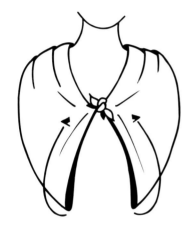

3 Now lift the lower front upwards…

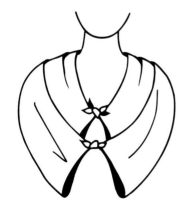

4 … and tie the upper corners using a Basic Knot.

These parallel knots can be worn at the front, or cheekily towards one side.

TIE - BABY

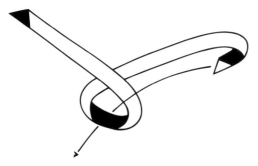

1 Fold the scarf into a narrow ribbon or into a cravat. Then tie a slip knot into the middle.

2 Pull the knot closed without tightening it and position the scarf around your neck, the knot to the front.

3 Tie it at the back with a Basic Knot.

1 Use a long scarf. Tie a loose knot into the longer end.

2 Thread the other end loosely through the centre of this knot.

3 Bring the knot into the desired position by pulling the shorter end downwards.

Alexa's Necklace

1 Hitch a slightly longer end over a shorter one.

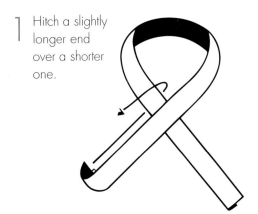

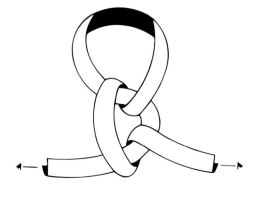

4 Tighten the knot by pulling both ends horizontally in opposite directions.

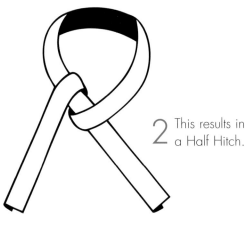

2 This results in a Half Hitch.

3 Tie another Half Hitch over the lower end.

5 Gently pull the straight, flat centre into a more decorative, wider shape. Then tie the ends at the back of your neck, using the Basic Knot.

Hair Care

Tie A Ribbon In Your Hair...

Long hair, short hair, wet hair... a ribbon is always a cheerful addition.

A colourful scarf will also protect your hair from bleaching sunrays or shelter it from the teasing winds.

On the following pages we present the greatest hits in 'hair-care'.

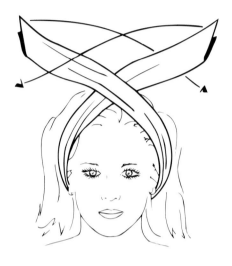

1 Wrap the folded scarf around your head, from the back to the front.

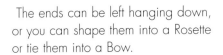

3 Tie the ends, using a Basic Knot.

The ends can be left hanging down, or you can shape them into a Rosette or tie them into a Bow.

2 Twist the ends around each other at the top and bring them to the back of your head.

Twin Coloured Ribbon

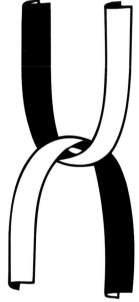

1 Lay out two ribbons so that they form the shape of a cross.

2 Lift the lower ribbon by its ends. The two ribbons will loop around each other.

3 Wrap them around your head. Tie them at the back, using a Basic Knot. The ends can be left hanging down, or, if you prefer, you can tuck them underneath the ribbon.

Sindbad The Sailor

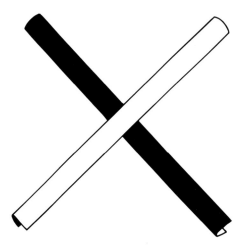

1 Lay out two ribbons so that they form the shape of a cross.

2 Lift the lower ribbon by its ends. The two ribbons will loop around each other.

3 Tie as for the Twin-Coloured Ribbons. Then loosen out and widen the ribbons by gently pulling them into a turban shape.

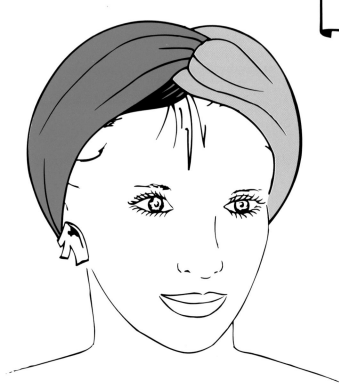

1 Twist your folded scarf into a rope.

2 Depending on the length of this rope, tie three to five knots into it.

3 Wrap the rope around your head and tie it at the back, using a Basic Knot.

GRACE KELLY

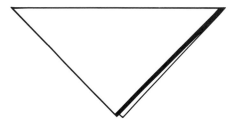

1   Fold your scarf into a triangle

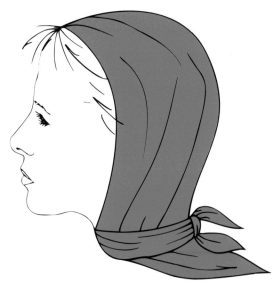

2   Lay it over your head.

3   Cross the corners at the front.

4   Tie the corners at the back, using a Basic Knot.

A little secret: If you pull the hood back off your head and gently shape the scarf at your neck you get a very nice design, which also looks good when turned around. The knot remains hidden. Of course, should the weather get bad you can always pull the hood up again.

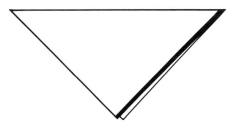

1 Fold your scarf into a triangle.

2 Lay it across your forehead, bringing it from the front, and twist the corners to form ropes.

3 Use a Basic Knot to tie the rope-shaped corners above the tip of your scarf at the back of your neck.

CORSAIR

1 Fold a square scarf in half and lift it by two opposite ends.

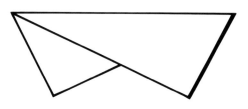

2 This results in two triangles, one on top of the other.

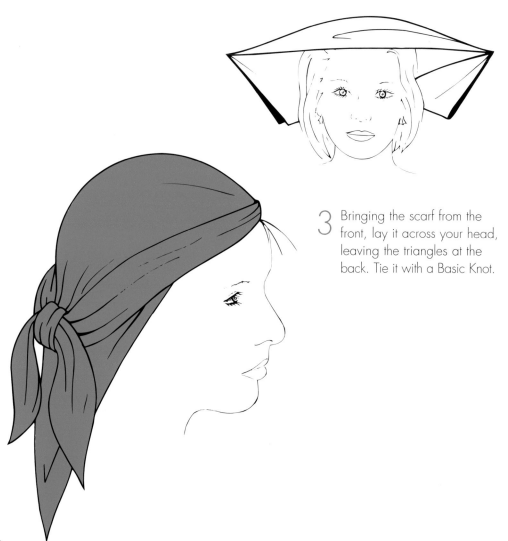

3 Bringing the scarf from the front, lay it across your head, leaving the triangles at the back. Tie it with a Basic Knot.

Gather your hair into a ponytail. Wrap a scarf once tightly around the base of this ponytail and, together with your hair, twist it to form a rope until the ponytail begins to coil. Then use some long hairpins to keep the bun in position.

Sunshade

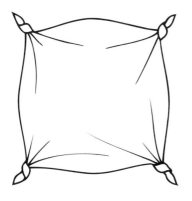

Take a rectangular scarf and tie a knot into each one of its four corners. Then place the scarf over your head.

Ballerina

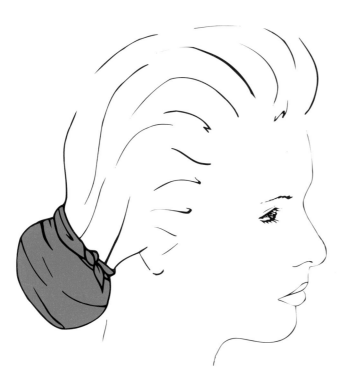

Gather your hair into a ponytail. Catch this ponytail in a scarf as you would in a small bag and tie the scarf at the base.

LOVELY HAIR IN FOCUS

Twist a scarf into a rope and wrap it, one or more times, around your forehead.

Elegant And Pretty

Dress up your hair, using an elegant bow.

(See pages 64 to 66).

On The Beach

Gather your hair into a ponytail. Knot a ribbon around its base and plait both ends into the ponytail. Tie the remaining ribbon ends into a bow.

Rosy Elegance

Tie a scarf around your head and twist the ends into a Rose.

(See page 58).

Pretty Cheeky

Knot a scarf around your head and tie the ends into a Fan.

(See pages 70 to 82).

Tip Top Fashion

Twist a scarf and a string of pearls into a rope and knot it around your head.

The Sporty Style

Wrap the centre of a ribbon around the base of your ponytail. Divide the ponytail into two halves and wrap each half into its appropriate portion of the ribbon.

Waist Wraps

Scarves make clever belts. You can roll them, weave them, plait them, crochet them or loop them through each other. They look smart just pulled through the belt loops, cheeky if tied to these same loops, adding a touch of cheerful colour, or they hint at romance if tied into an elegant bow.

Try it for yourself…

You will find lots of ideas on the following pages.

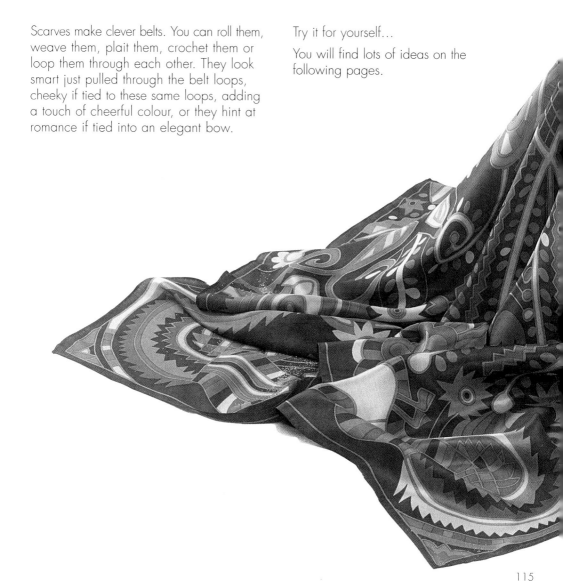

CALYPSO

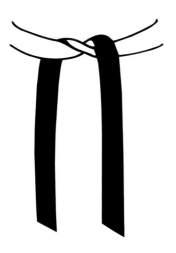

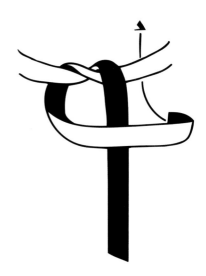

1 Wrap a long scarf around your waist and make a Half Hitch.

2 Bring the lower end above the upper one.

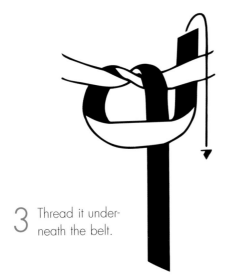

3 Thread it underneath the belt.

4 Repeat these steps with the other end, and keep repeating.

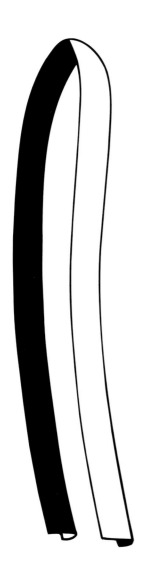

2 Wrap it around your waist and pull the two ends through the loop. Hold the belt in position with a Loopholder (p. 47).

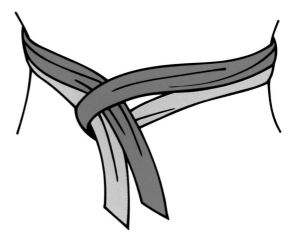

3 Or secure it with a Woven Loop (p. 44).

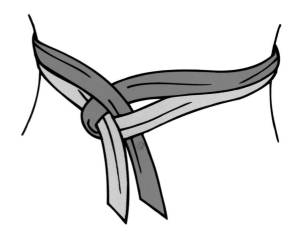

1 Halve a long scarf lengthways.

CROCHET BELT

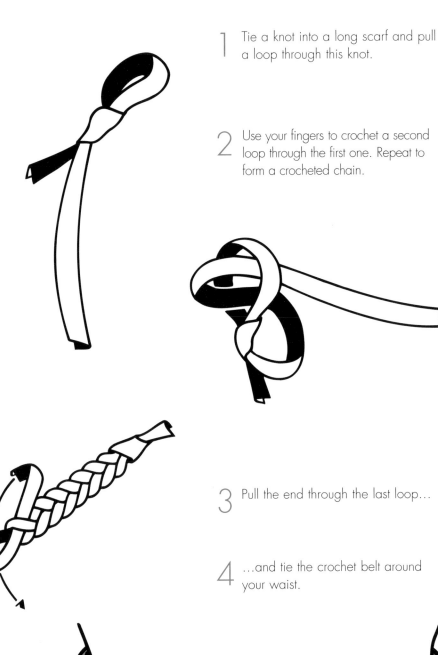

1 Tie a knot into a long scarf and pull a loop through this knot.

2 Use your fingers to crochet a second loop through the first one. Repeat to form a crocheted chain.

3 Pull the end through the last loop...

4 ...and tie the crochet belt around your waist.

Your Waistline

In Focus

11 Clever Ways To Belt Up

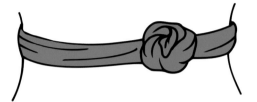

Use a long scarf as a belt and shape the ends to form a Rose (p. 58).

Twist a long scarf into a rope and use this as a belt.

Join three scarves and plait them into a tri-coloured belt.

Tie a simple knot into a folded scarf. Place it around your waist, the knot at the front, and tie it at the back, using a Basic Knot.

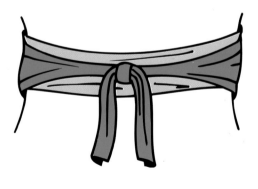

Wrap a long scarf around your waist, from the front to the back. Cross the ends at the back and bring them to the front. Then tie, using a Basic Knot.

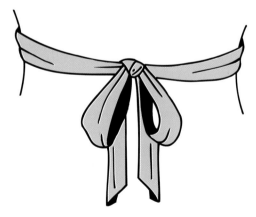

Wrap a long scarf around your waist, starting at the back. Tie the front ends into a decorative bow.

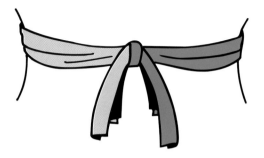

Loop two scarves through each other and tie the ends at the back…

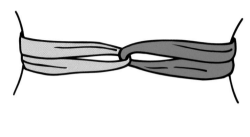

…or, if you prefer, tie them at the front.

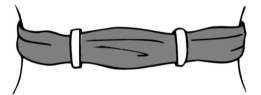

Thread a scarf through your belt loops …

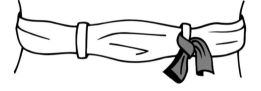

… or tie a kerchief to one of these loops.

Thread two colour co-ordinated scarves through your belt loops and tie them, front and back, with a Basic Knot.

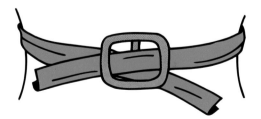

Thread both ends of a scarf through a buckle.

TOPS - DELIGHTFUL

AND DISCREET

Delightful to view and yet discreet. That's what you will be when wearing your scarf as a bikini-top. Not only will you look smart, but everyone will also watch with interest to see if the top will stay in place!

Experiment until you find which style looks nicest with your figure. And you will be surprised - these wraps fit better than you might expect.

1 Take a long wide scarf or fold a thin shawl four times.

2 Position the scarf from your back to your front and cross the ends halfway up your chest.

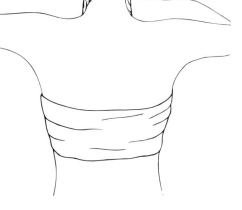

3 Twist the ends into tight ropes and tie them at the back of your neck, using the Basic Knot.

RIMINI

1 Tie a slip knot into the centre of your scarf.

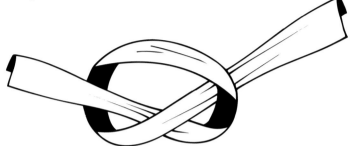

2 Pull this knot tight.

3 Position this knot in front and tie the ends at the back, using a Basic Knot.

1 Form a triangle out of two scarves.

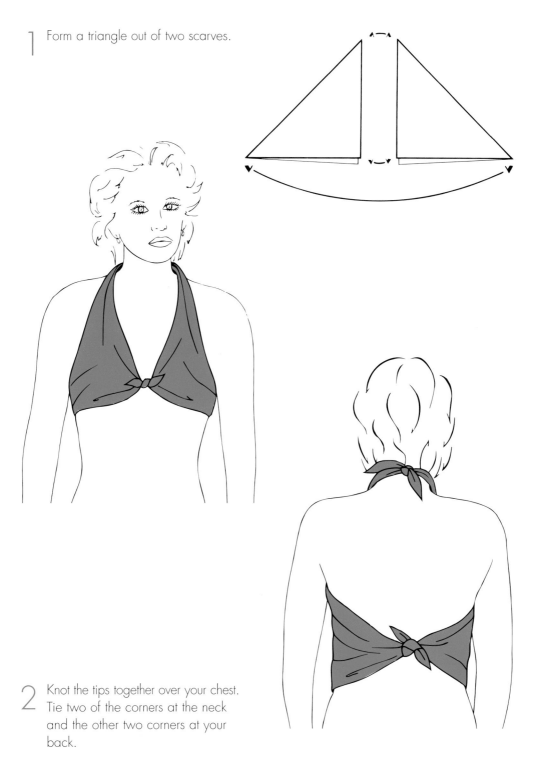

2 Knot the tips together over your chest. Tie two of the corners at the neck and the other two corners at your back.

TOULON

1 Fold two scarves into cravates.

2 Tie them together with a Basic Knot.

3 Position the scarves at the front across your chest and tie them at the back, using the Basic Knot.

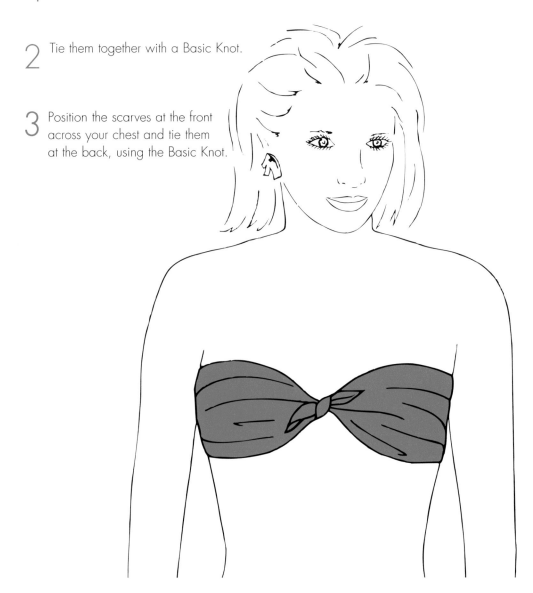

1 Wrap a scarf around your chest and tie it beneath one arm, using a Basic Knot.

2 Loop the other ends over your shoulder, one from the front and one from the back. Tie them at the top with another Basic Knot.

1 Wrap a scarf around your chest and tie it with a Basic Knot at the back.

2 Thread a second scarf under the first one, approximately halfway across your chest. Tie this at the back of your neck, using a Basic Knot.

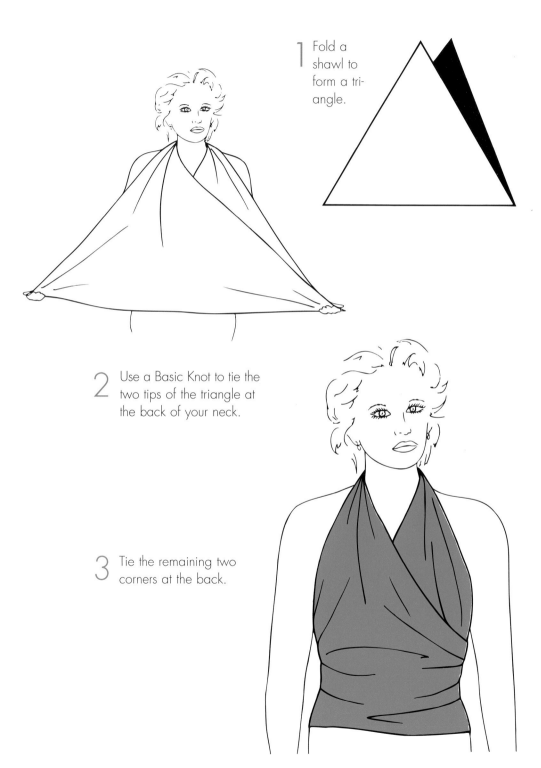

1 Fold a shawl to form a tri-angle.

2 Use a Basic Knot to tie the two tips of the triangle at the back of your neck.

3 Tie the remaining two corners at the back.

Sun Top

1 Take a big, soft, square shawl.

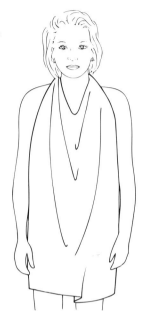

2 Tie two ends at the neck.

3 Roll up the lower edges of the shawl to waist height.

4 Tie the rolled up ends at the back.

Tops And Tails

1 Hold a large, soft shawl near its centre and leave it to hang down loosely.

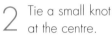

2 Tie a small knot at the centre.

3 Hold the shawl at two parallel ends, A and B.

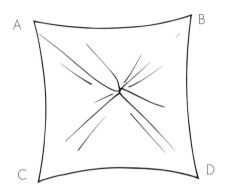

4 Tie corners A and B at the neck, using an inward pointing Basic Knot.

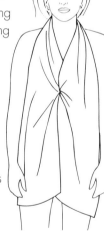

5 Twist corners C and D into ropes and tie them at your back.

PAREO - HAWAIIAN DREAM

The pareo is a magical, multifaceted item of clothing just right for the sunny side of life.

A hot day on the beach or at the pool will see this simple scarf transformed into a cleverly designed dress, into an airy eyecatcher, into a refreshing summery wraparound top or into some other fashionable figure.

What is the secret of these transformations? For inspiration see the following pages!

Hawaii

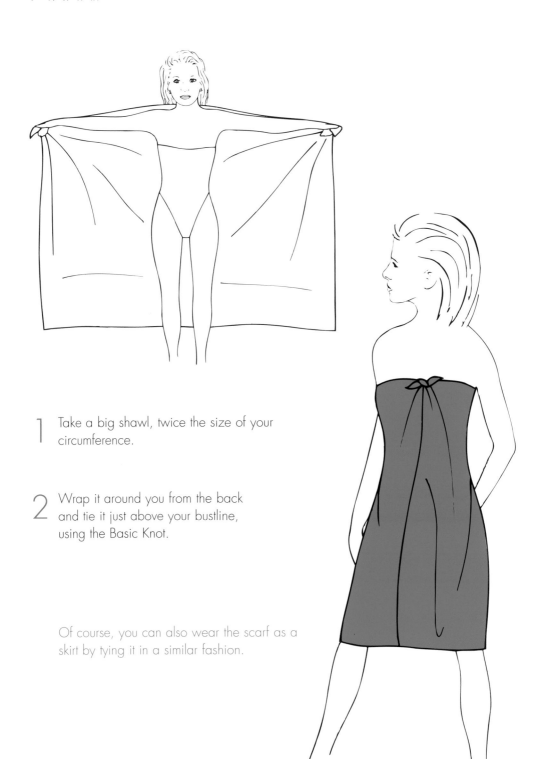

1 Take a big shawl, twice the size of your circumference.

2 Wrap it around you from the back and tie it just above your bustline, using the Basic Knot.

Of course, you can also wear the scarf as a skirt by tying it in a similar fashion.

1 Take a large, soft Pareo, twice the size of your circumference.

4 Use your armpits to hold the Pareo both right and left at points X. Bring both tips A and B to your chest, where they can be tied, using the Basic Knot.

2 Fold it in half, leaving the portion at the back 15 cm longer than the front.

This way of tying the Pareo has advantages. Because the 15 cms have been folded over the front edge there is no unsightly opening. Instead, the front forms an attractive and comfortable pleat.

Tied at your waist the Pareo can also be worn as a skirt.

3 Fold these 15 cm over the front edge.

TONGA

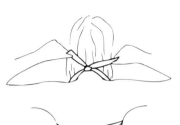

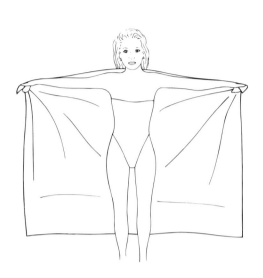

2 Loosely tie the two corners at the back of your neck.

1 Take a large shawl, twice the width of your body. Lay it across your back. Bring the upper corners beneath your arms and towards the front.

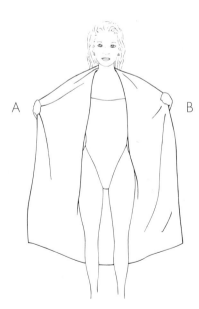

A   B

4 ...and tie points A and B above your chest, using a Basic Knot.

3 Extend the shawl to its full width at around waist height...

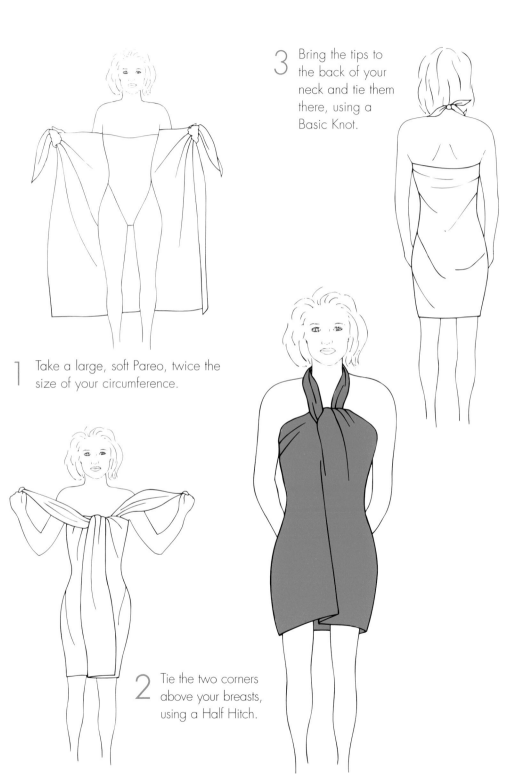

3 Bring the tips to the back of your neck and tie them there, using a Basic Knot.

1 Take a large, soft Pareo, twice the size of your circumference.

2 Tie the two corners above your breasts, using a Half Hitch.

Bahamas

Tied at your waist the Pareo can also be worn as a skirt.

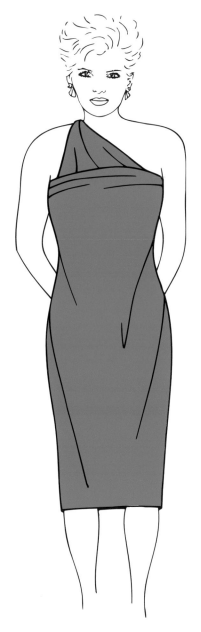

1 Wrap the Pareo once around yourself above your breasts, starting at the front.
Hold on to the upper corner above your right shoulder.

2 Wrap the shawl around yourself once more, again staying above your breasts.

3 Tie the two corners at your shoulder, using the Basic Knot.

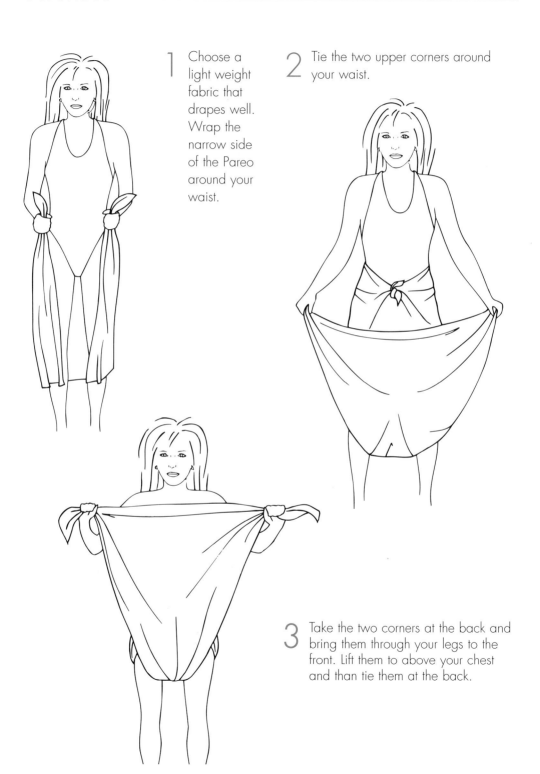

1 Choose a light weight fabric that drapes well. Wrap the narrow side of the Pareo around your waist.

2 Tie the two upper corners around your waist.

3 Take the two corners at the back and bring them through your legs to the front. Lift them to above your chest and than tie them at the back.

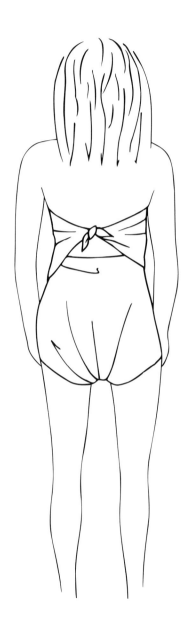
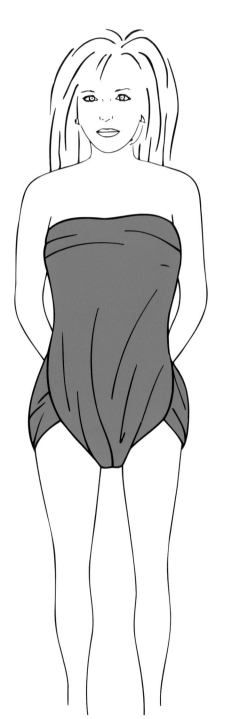

SAMOA

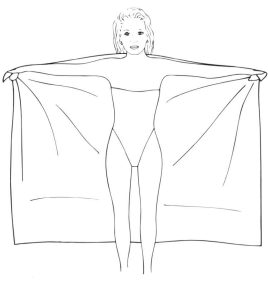

1 Take a large shawl, twice the size of your circumference.

2 Lay it across your back. Bring it beneath your arms towards the front. Cross the ends and tie the corners behind your neck.

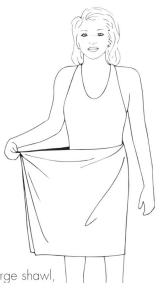

1 Take a large shawl, twice the size of your circumference, fold it in half and wrap it around your waist. Fold the two open edges towards your waist.

2 Fold the shawl once more until…

3 …it fits tightly around your waist. Turn the upper edge inwards, rolling it over twice.

SKIRT

1 Take two scarves of complimentary
colours, large enough to wrap
around your waist.

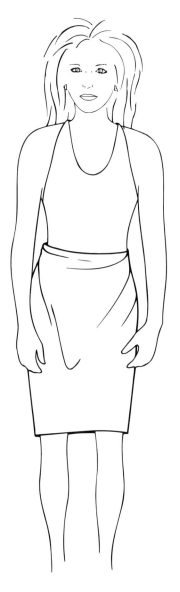

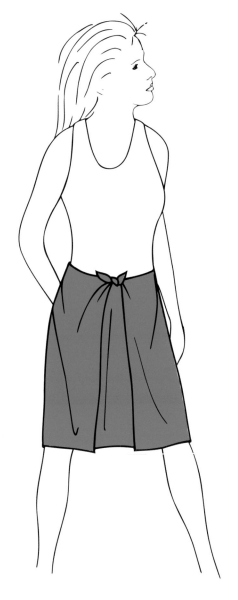

2 Wrap one scarf from the front to the
back around your waist and tie it at
the back, using a Basic Knot.

3 Wrap the second scarf around your
waist from the back to the front and tie
it at the front, again using a Basic Knot.

1 Take two scarves of complimentary
colours, each large enough to wrap
around your waist.

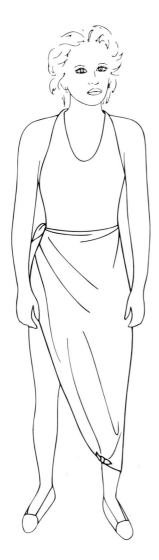

2 Place the first scarf around your hips.
Tie the corners at one hip, using a
Basic Knot. Then tie the corners at
the opposite ankle, again using a
Basic Knot.

3 Tie the second scarf just like the first
one, at the other side.

Pocket Hankies

Some people tie a knot in their hanky to remind them of something they don't want to forget.

Years ago ladies dropped it inadvertently - to blushingly receive it back from the hands of a gallant admirer.

The following designs will show you how to spirit a fashionable spot of colour into the breastpocket of your blazer.

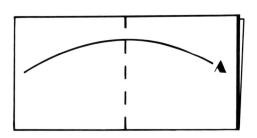

Pocket Handkerchiefs add style to men's and women's outfits alike. The ideal dimension is 30cm x 30cm.

1 Fold the kerchief in half…

2 … and halve this again.

3 Hold the kerchief at the centre (point X) and gently pull out the four loose ends.

X

4 Fold the centre tip up.

5 Either just allow the four tips to peep out…

6 … or the four tips and the top of the centre tip…

7 … or just the top of the centre tip.

SUGGESTION: Why not use 2 or 3 kerchiefs of complimentary colours and stick them into your breastpocket at the same time?

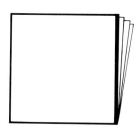

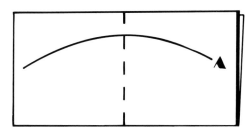

1 Fold a kerchief in half…

2 … and halve it again.

X

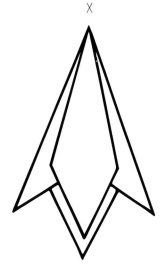

3 Hold the kerchief at the centre (point X) and pull the four corners into decorative shapes.

4 Use a brooch or a pin to attach the kerchief onto your lapel.

149

ROSE - BROOCH

1 Fold a kerchief into a narrow ribbon or into a tie. Tie a knot in the centre.

2 The two ends should have the same length. Wrap them around each other to form a rope.

3 Keep twisting the rope till it forms a coil.

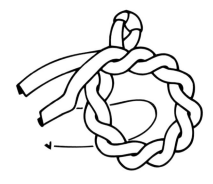

4 Shape a small fold out of one-of the ends and pull this through the centre of the coil.

5 Allow the tips to protrude like leaves and use a safety pin to attach the Rose to your lapel.

GIGANTIC IDEAS FOR LARGE SCARVES, PASHMINAS AND SHAWLS

With clever covers, even the coldest days won't see you cold shouldered.

Add colour to your outfit by draping them over your coat in winter, or wear them in spring and autumn as a most attractive coat-substitute. The next ten ideas are, of course, not only for cold days!

Huge scarves are ideal for the barbecue outside, if the evening turns chilly.

Wrap yourself in shawls, pashminas and scarves to your heart's delight. The following pages leave you ten times as well covered.

Davos

1 Fold a big shawl into a triangle
or use a pashmina.

Tied like this, the shawl across
your shoulders is guaranteed not
to slip.

2 Lay it across your shoulders.

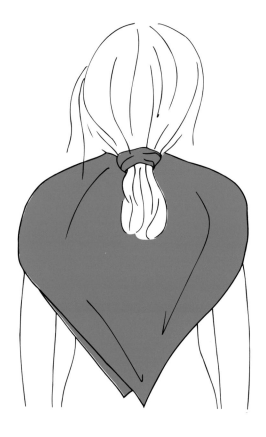

3 Bring the tips from the front, under your
arms, to the back and tie them there,
using a Basic Knot.

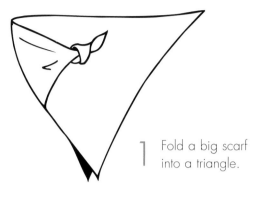

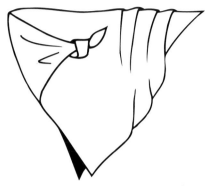

2 Tie a knot into one of the tips.

1 Fold a big scarf into a triangle.

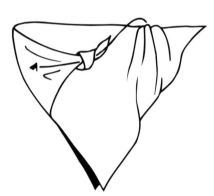

3 Lay the triangle across your shoulders. Create a few creases just above the other tip.

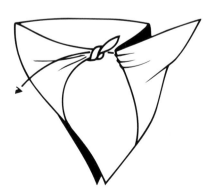

4 Gather these creases together and push them through the centre of the knot.

St. Tropez

1   Fold a shawl to form a triangle, or use a pashmina.

2   Lay it across your shoulders and tie the front corners using a Basic Knot.

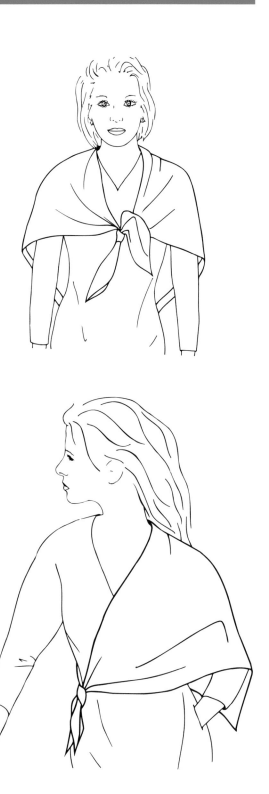

3   Push that knot casually onto your shoulder…

4   …or wear it at your waist.

Allassio

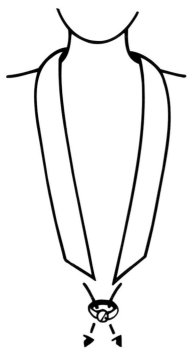

1 Fold a big scarf or shawl to form a cravat.

2 Lay this cravat across your shoulders and pull the ends through an attractive toggle or ring.

3 For a casual look, throw one of the ends across your shoulder.

1 Fold a shawl in half.

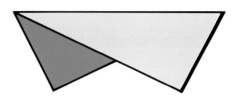

2 Hold the shawl at two opposite ends.
This will result in two triangles.

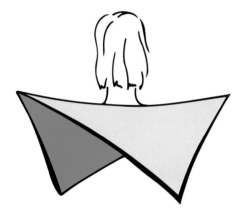

3 Lay the shawl across your shoulders,
the triangles at the back.

4 Tie it with a nice brooch in front...

5 ... or tie it as in the Butterfly (see
p. 158, picture 3).

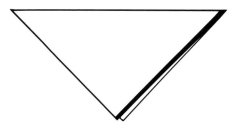

1 Fold a scarf to form a triangle.

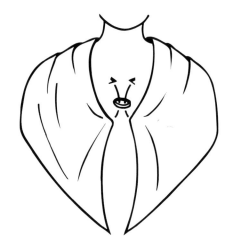

2 Lay it across your shoulders.

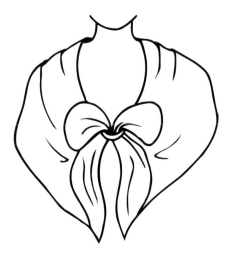

3 Catch the inner edges halfway down. Push these through a toggle, a nice ring or a buckle.

4 Gently pull the newly formed tips into the shape of two butterfly wings.

Bolero

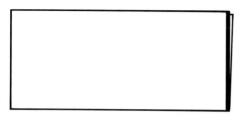

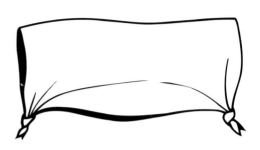

1 Fold a large square in half, with the outer side of the shawl turned inwards.

2 Slip knot both ends of loose corners. Tie both ends, using a Basic Knot.

3 Turn the shawl inside out. Now the knots are facing inwards.

4 Lay it across your shoulders and bring your arms through the two openings. The knots should be placed below your arms.

1   Fold a shawl to form a triangle.

2   Lay it across your shoulders and tuck
    the corners at the front underneath
    your belt.
    This is also suitable for pashminas.

LARA

Fold a shawl or pashmina into an oblong.

Lay it across one shoulder and tuck both ends, front and back, underneath your belt.

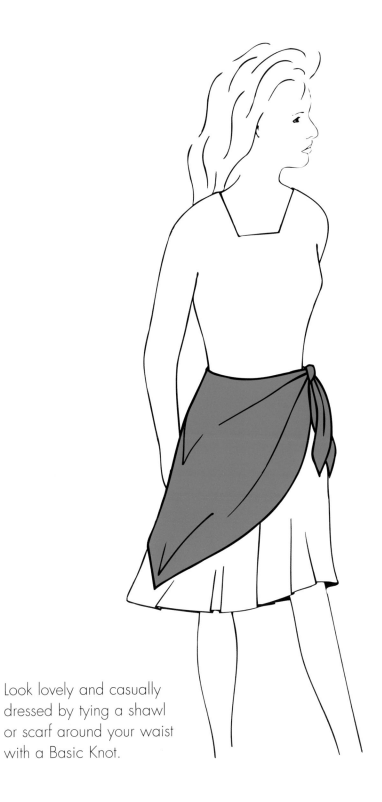

Look lovely and casually dressed by tying a shawl or scarf around your waist with a Basic Knot.

Scarves For Children

Both Cute And Cheeky

Babies and toddlers burn quickly when exposed to the sun, so they need protection. Playing on the beach, sailing in a boat or during any other sunny adventure they will be safely covered when wearing a scarf. Scarves are invaluable where little girls are concerned, for a cheerful blob of colour at the neck, or for a really clever decoration in their hair.

Take two scarves of equal size and fold each to form a triangle. Tie the tips at the front and the back, using the Basic Knot.

Plait a scarf made out of a thin fabric into your daughter's pigtails …

… and pin them to the top of her head.

A pirate's headscarf looks smart on both boys and girls (see p. 107).

Take a scarf and tie an attractive bow into your daughter's hair.

Scarves For Gentlemen

Do men use scarves?

When I think about it I can initially only picture the obligatory tie, which many men think of as a necessary evil and which they discard the moment they come home.

Research by the English Association of Tie Manufacturers has established that a tie can tell a lot about the attitudes, mood and capability of the person wearing it.

The study came to the following conclusions:

Extrovert men wear colourful ties with eyecatching patterns. A tie with light and dark stripes of the same width suggests that the wearer is of an indecisive character. Optimistic men, and those who like people, prefer a broad stripe on a dark background. Pessimists like exactly the opposite.

Men who have had an unhappy past choose multicoloured ties. Car dealers like lightly coloured ties with dark dots. Conservative gents wear a paisley pattern. Organised men prefer dark, geometrically shaped patterns on a light background.

You probably have your own ideas about the connection between the type of tie someone chooses and their character. But it is a fact that the tie is the only bit of colour men are allowed to wear with what is often a very drab everyday outfit.

So this accessory allows men to underscore their individuality and their special characteristics. Colour is not the only factor that counts, though it should, of course, suit its wearer.

The fabric, too, says something about your character and type. A wide tie made of tweed says you are easygoing and natural, as does a silk tie, either striped or with a diamond pattern.

A slightly shiny tie with a paisley pattern suggests elegance, especially if adorned by a smart tiepin.

Even on ordinary days it looks smart to wear a kerchief in your breastpocket, its colours matching your tie. Why should this kerchief only be allowed on special occasions?

And then there are, of course, the obligatory scarves for winter, which are worn to keep the cold out. Tied with a Half Hitch they usually fulfil this purpose.

But – have a look – there are also other ways to tie your woolly scarf.

THE NARROW KNOT

FOR RIGHT-HANDED PEOPLE

THE KNOT IS SMALL AND LONG

All drawings are inverted. Position the book in front of you against a mirror and tie exactly as depicted in the diagrams

1 Put the tie around your neck. The wide end should be around 30cm longer than the narrow one and should lie over your right shoulder.

2 Bring the wide end across the narrow one and wrap it once around the narrow end.

3 Bring the wide end across the narrow one once more. This will form a loop.

4 Bring the wide end from the bottom to the top and thread it through the noose at your neck and through the loop.

5 Use one hand to tighten the knot by pulling at the narrow end while positioning the knot precisely at the centre of your collar with the other hand.

The tie is perfectly knotted if the tip of the wide end just touches the belt of your trousers.

For Right-Handed People

The Knot Is Somewhat Triangular

All drawings are inverted. Position the book in front of you against a mirror and tie exactly as depicted in the diagrams

1 Put the tie around your neck. The wide end should be around 30 cm longer than the narrow one and should lie over your right shoulder.

2 Bring the wide end across the narrow one and wrap it once around the narrow end.

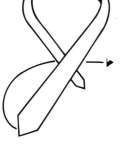

3 Bring the wide end across the narrow one and through the noose at your neck.

4 Bring the wide end across the narrow one once more. This will form a loop.

5 Bring the wide end from the bottom through the noose at your neck and then from the top through the loop.

Use one hand to tighten the knot by pulling at the narrow end while positioning the knot precisely at the centre of your collar with the other hand.

The tie is perfectly knotted if the tip of the wide end just touches the belt of your trousers. The Half Windsor is somewhat bigger and more triangular than the Narrow Knot.

Windsor

For Right-handed People

This Results In A Big Knot

All drawings are inverted. Position the book in front of you against a mirror and tie exactly as depicted in the diagrams

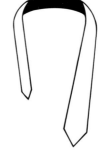

1 Put the tie around your neck. The wide end should be around 30cm longer than the narrow one and should lie over your right shoulder.

2 Bring the wide end across the narrow one and use it to make a Half Hitch.

3 Bring the wide end behind the narrow one, across the noose and then down behind the noose.

4 Bring the wide end across the narrow one once more. This will form a loop.

5 Bring the wide end from below, through the noose at your neck and from above through the loop.

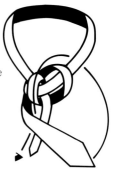

Use one hand to tighten the knot by pulling at the narrow end while positioning the knot precisely at the centre of your collar with the other hand.

In the good old days men kept a hanky scented with Eau de Cologne in their breastpocket in case it might be required to revive a fainting lady. Today it serves only decorative purposes.

But it is still worn in just the same stylish way, casually arranged in suitpockets, blazerpockets or even in the pocket of your shirt. (For instructions see p. 147)

THE DICKY BOW

All drawings are inverted. Position the book in front of you against a mirror and tie exactly as depicted in the diagrams

2 Fold the lower, short end.

1 Bring the longer, left end across the right one and push it underneath the noose.

3 Bring the upper, longer end across the centre…

4 … and fold the longer end as well.

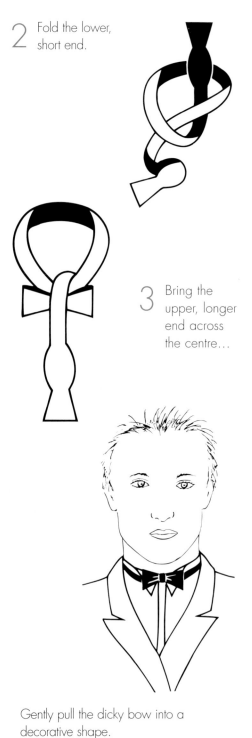

5 Push this second fold through the knot behind the first fold and pull the dicky bow tight.

Gently pull the dicky bow into a decorative shape.

LOOPED KNOT

This is a handy way to shorten an excessively long scarf.

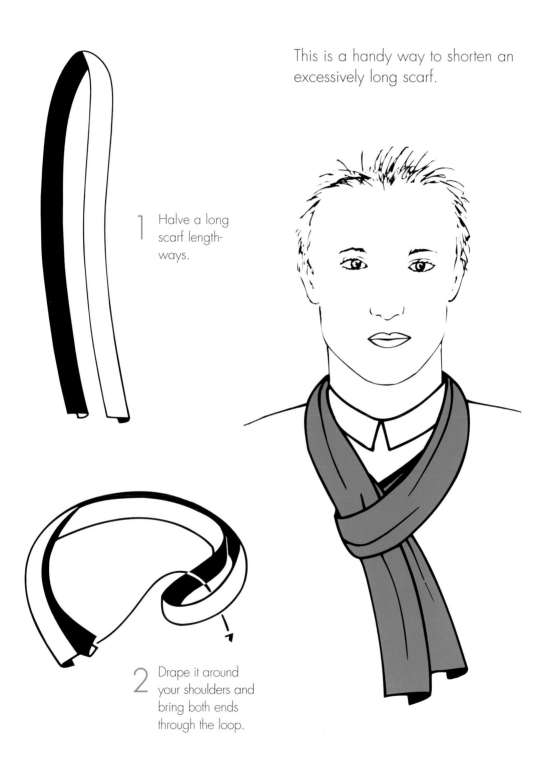

1 Halve a long scarf lengthways.

2 Drape it around your shoulders and bring both ends through the loop.

Woven Loop

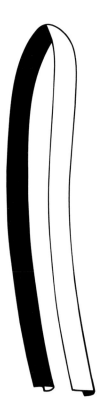

1   Halve a long scarf lengthways.

2   Bring it around your shoulders and thread the two ends through the loop, one end from the top and one end from the bottom.

3   Gently pull the scarf into a decorative shape.

These scarves look distinguished when worn inside the collar of your winter coat.

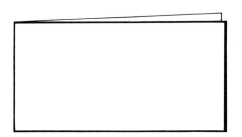

1   Halve a big scarf.

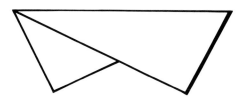

2   Hold it at two opposite ends. This will result in two triangles.

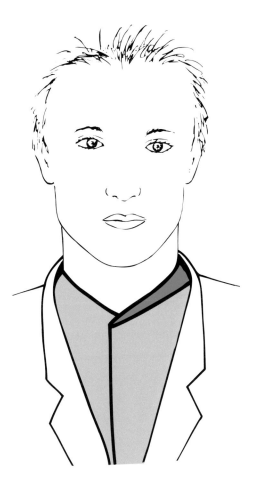

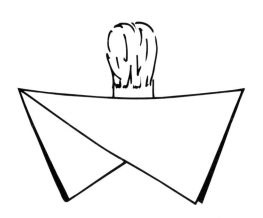

3   Lay the scarf across your shoulders, the triangles at the back.

4   Then cross it at the front.

Old Hat With New Charm

Scarves help to brighten up old hats. You choose whether to tilt your hat towards the classic, the elegant, the sporty, the romantic or the cute. A new plain hat will also enjoy this kind of facelift.

With the ends of the scarf extended in a long and flowing style.

Hats can be decorated:

With two scarves of complimentary colours, twisted into a rope p. 56).

With one scarf, twisted into a rope (p. 54).

With a Fan (p. 77).

With a pretty bow (p. 65).

With a Rosette (p. 68).

With a Rose (p. 58).

With scarf and pearls twisted into a rope (p. 85).

The Same Shoe, In 4 Magic Guises

With the use of special shoe clips and a little imagination a plain court shoe can be transformed into a magic slipper.

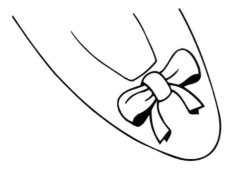

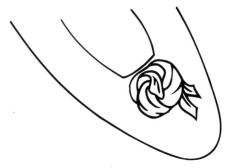

1 This little bow has got what it takes, especially if it colour co-ordinates with the rest of your outfit (p. 65).

2 It is amazing how, with this tiny fabric rose, a daytime court shoe becomes fit for evening wear (p. 58).

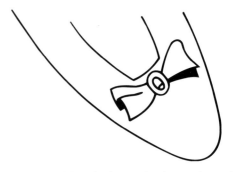

3 This small, airy fan lends a touch of elegance to your shoe (p. 77).

4 A small kerchief, simply drawn through a decorative belt buckle, transforms an old shoe into a new one.

POUCHES

Cute yet practical, for the essential small things in life.

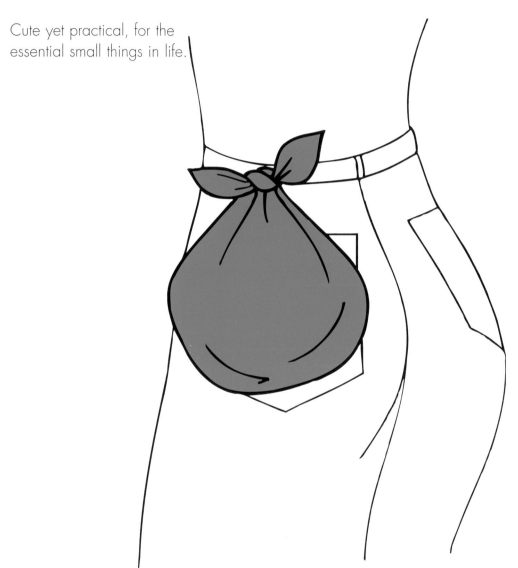

Knot the four corners of a scarf crossways and tie the pouch to one of your belt loops.

FANCY DRESS

Fancy Dress, hooray! But what will I wear?

It need not necessarily be an expensive or tailored outfit. A collection of scarves and shawls form the ideal starting position for a very individualistic costume. With just a few scarves you and your family can be quickly disguised.

- Why not try the Turkish Trousers (p. 145), in conjunction with a Tri Top (p. 129). Behold, the Sultan's wife has arrived!

- No pirate is complete without his headscarf (p. 107 - 108). This is also a popular idea with children.

- Hawaiian Dreams can be lived and expressed in different varieties – see from p.133 onwards.

- Wrap a number of large scarves once around a belt. The witches' skirt is ready. Next drape a shawl across your shoulder, as on p. 154, and put on a headscarf. Then head off to the witches' ball.

If you leaf through this book a bit longer you will surely find a few more fancy ideas.

THE MAGIC SCARF

The same scarf – 4 different ways!

Paint your own scarf on silk. Here are just a few ideas.

- Divide a large scarf into four even squares.
- Paint each square with a different colour as background.
- Make sure that all colours compliment each other.

- Draw imaginative, similar designs, again taking care that all colours compliment each other.
- One of the background colours will become the dominant one, depending on how you fold your scarf. It can thus be worn in an extremely varied way with a large number of different outfits.

Light Blue

Pink

Purple

Bottle Green

Home - Made Shawls And Scarves

If you are on good terms with a needle and thread, or if you own a sewing machine, you will find it quite easy to run up some attractive scarves that will compliment and highlight your wardrobe. All you need is some straight seams, and already you have a multifaceted fashionable accessory.

Here are a few hints:

● Most shops will sell scarves of the same pattern, but different colours, for little money. Join two or three of these to form a new, interesting scarf.

● Combine a thin, patterned fabric with a thin plain one by stitching them together, right side on right side, leaving only a small opening. (The fabric lengths can vary from 1.3m to 2.5m, as you prefer.) Use the opening to turn the finished sewing inside out and then stitch it up by hand. Result: A clever scarf, made even cuter by the addition of a fringe.

● Skirt: Stitch together two ready made scarves you have bought (dimensions approx. 55x55cm) , right side on right side, along two of the long sides. Leave approx. 17cm on one side as a slit. Turn the right sides out and admire your new miniskirt.

Order Form

Dear Mrs. Keller-Krische,

Your suggestions and tips on how to tie scarves in imaginative ways have given me many ideas on improving my appearance.

Please send me ＿＿ book(s)

THE BOOK OF SCARVES: 100 IDEAS SCARVES, SHAWLS AND TIES DRESSED WITH IMAGINATION - at the price of Euro 16,50 VAT incl.

Delivery will be by mail, postage added.

Name: _____

Address: _____

Date and Signature: _____

THE BOOK OF SCARVES: 100 IDEAS
is available in all good bookstores, or alter-
natively cut out this page and send it to:

Christiane Keller-Krische
c/o 'White Horses'
Kilcolta
Myrtleville
Co. Cork
Rep. of Ireland

Or by tel/fax
From Rep. of Ireland   0 21 4831511
From outside Ireland   00 353 21 4831511

e-mail: **info@keller-krische.de**
Internet: www.keller-krische.de

(Prices subject to change without notice)